Straw Hats

&

Bonnets

Joan Curran

The
Book
Castle

First published October 2003
by The Book Castle
12 Church Street, Dunstable LU5 4RU

Designed and Typeset by Priory Graphics, Flitwick, Bedfordshire

Printed by Antony Rowe Limited, Chippenham, Wiltshire

OLD TRADES OF DUNSTABLE SERIES
Previous Titles

Colin Bourne *Dales' Dubbin and Flemons' Herbs* **(1996)**

Don Kemp & Fred Moore *Shops & Markets* **(1997)**

Joan Curran *The Whiting Works* **(1998)**

Colin Bourne *Bagshawe's and Cross Paperware* **(2000)**

ISBN 1-903747-45-7

CONTENTS

FOREWORD

'Straw Hats and Bonnets' is not a history of the cottage industry of straw plaiting, but the story of the Dunstable hat manufacturers of the 19th century, when hats were made in factories and the industry was the mainstay of the economy of the town. It begins in the late eighteenth century and ends in the early twentieth. Over those years there were many hat factories in Dunstable, ranging from small family concerns to large firms employing three to four hundred people. Some had only a short existence, others survived for over a century.

To trace the history of each and every one in detail is beyond the scope of a small book such as this. The first part of the book is therefore a general history of the industry in Dunstable from 1785 to 1931, when the last factory closed. The second part is in the form of a hat trail, in which you will find the individual stories of the thirteen major firms who were manufacturing hats when the trade was at its peak, in the 1870s and early 1880s.

This is the fifth book in the series 'The Old Trades of Dunstable' and, like the other four, it had its beginnings in one of the Dunstable and District Local History Society's 'Trades Evenings'. We hope you will find it as interesting and enjoyable as the previous four have proved to be.

Joan Curran

ACKNOWLEDGEMENTS

The Society and the author would like to thank all those people who have helped in any way in the production of this book. In particular our thanks are due to Rita Swift for the many hours spent searching through past issues of the Dunstable Gazette, to David Cheshire for collating and analysing statistics from the 1851 census and to the staff at Luton Museum for their invaluable help.

THE AUTHOR

Joan Curran is a founder member of the Dunstable & District Local History Society and has served as Secretary since its inauguration in 1992. She is also an active member of the Bedfordshire Historical Records Society and the Bedfordshire Local History Association and serves on the User Panel of the Bedfordshire & Luton Archives and Records Service (formerly the Bedfordshire County Record Office).

PART I

THE STORY OF AN INDUSTRY
1785 - 1931

From Cottage to Factory

The making of hats from straw plait almost certainly originated in Italy, in Tuscany, in the 16th century. Though there are several theories about its origin in this country there is no conclusive evidence as to how it arrived here. Perhaps immigrants or refugees from the Continent brought their skills over here, or travellers brought Italian hats back home with them and they were copied by the English women. There is even a possibility that English straw plaiting was actually a development of an older native skill. Whichever way it was, straw hats were certainly becoming items of fashion in the 17th century and in the 18th century Dunstable bonnets were mentioned for the first time. Per Kalm, a Swedish visitor who stayed at the Robin Hood Inn in Little Gaddesden in 1748, describing how the local women were dressed, wrote that, 'When they go out they always wear straw hats which they have made themselves from wheat straw and they are pretty enough'.

It was in the South East Midlands, and particularly in Bedfordshire and North Hertfordshire, that straw plaiting and hat making eventually became concentrated, perhaps because of their proximity to London and the turnpike roads. Travellers journeying to and from the North on the Watling Street frequently commented on the selling of hats and other articles made of straw-boxes, baskets and toys etc. – at Dunstable. The plaiters would offer their wares for sale in the porch of the Sugar Loaf and it was even said that the windows on the ground floor were made so that sales could be made through the open windows. Hat markets were also held in several of the local towns, such as Hemel Hempstead, where the takings for straw hats were reported to have reached as much as £200 in one day.

But from the early 1600s English hat makers began to find themselves up against foreign competition as London merchants started importing hats from Italy. Italian straw being much finer than English straw, the finished hats were naturally much more elegant, and though the English hats were widely worn in the countryside, and probably in the less wealthy parts of the capital, the fashionable ladies of London preferred Leghorns, as the Italian imports came to be known.

Even so, plaiting increasingly provided a valuable source of income for the women of this area. Although one commentator in the 1760s wrote that 'not a great deal of hands are employed by it', a little later others were reporting that it was an important part of the local economy and most of the women (and many children) were involved in the trade by the end of the century. It was said in 1810 that women in Bedfordshire could earn from six to twelve shillings a week from plaiting in the busy season and children from three to four shillings. When a new master was wanted for the Dunstable poorhouse in 1813 the Overseers advertised for 'a proper person who understands the Straw Manufactory'.

Up until the late 18th century the making of straw hats had been solely a cottage industry. Plaiters working on their own, or together in families, had bleached their own straw and plaited it, sewn the plait into hats, stiffened and blocked them and taken them to town to sell. However, things were about to change, and two events occurred which acted as a catalyst that would bring about this change.

The first of these was the outbreak of the Napoleonic Wars in Europe, which inevitably meant a drastic decline in trade with the Continent. Very few hats now could be imported from Italy and heavy import duties were imposed on plait and hats that did get through, making them very expensive (though the smuggling of both hats and plait was by no means unknown). There was therefore a ready market just waiting to be exploited.

Fortuitously it was at about the same time that somebody invented a little tool that was to make a huge difference to the making of straw plait. This was the straw splitter, with which one straw could be split into a number of very fine splits, or strips. As with the introduction of the craft of straw plaiting, there is more than one story about how, and by whom, it was invented. One story is that splitters made of bone were invented by prisoners of war at Yaxley, near Peterborough. Another says that Mr Janes, a blacksmith of Dunstable, invented a splitter made of iron, while another version says that Mr Janes only improved on a design invented by another blacksmith. Whichever is the correct version, the splitter was like a very small, slender pencil, with a sharp, fluted point which could be inserted into one end of a hollow straw and pushed through so that the straw was split into a number of narrow strips. The improved version had the handle at right angles to the point, making it easier to use, and later still brass was used instead of iron. The great advantage of this invention was that a much finer plait could now be made which could rival that of the Italian merchants. One of the Dunstable manufacturers was said to have been the first person to have produced hats made of split straw commercially and to have made £10,000 in one year alone.

The end of the 18th century also saw the beginning of the Industrial Revolution and in the north of England the textile industries were already moving from cottage to factory. Though not driven by the invention of machinery to do the work previously done by hand, as was the case in the north, the straw hat trade gradually followed their example. In 1785, in an early directory, there appeared an entry for the first person in the town to be described as a hat manufacturer.

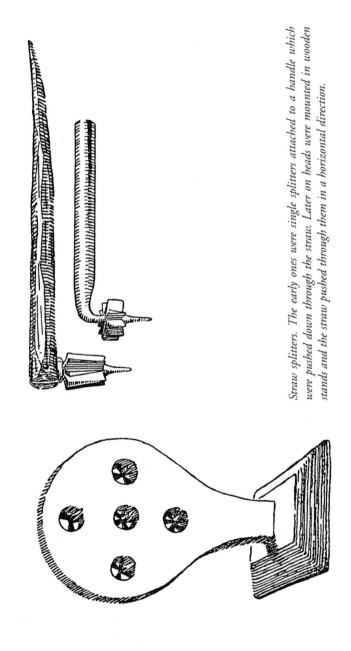

Straw splitters. The early ones were single splitters attached to a handle which were pushed down through the straw. Later on heads were mounted in wooden stands and the straw pushed through them in a horizontal direction.

The gentleman referred to was Mark Brown (his name is incorrectly given as Broom), described as manufacturer of hats and haberdasher. Property deeds refer to him as occupying premises 'formerly an inn... known as the Saracen's Head' and it is possible that this is where he had his factory. This was not the Saracen's Head that we know today, but stood on the site of Albion Buildings, in High Street South, where William Hill's betting shop is now. Certainly the premises were later used as a hat factory run by the Waterfield family for many years, until they were given notice to quit by the owner. Wherever his factory was, Mark Brown was followed in the business by his son, William Frederick Brown, the man who made the aforementioned £10,000.

A draper who was also for a time a straw hat manufacturer was William Elliott (not to be confused with his nephew and namesake, who would later be the owner of one of the largest factories in the town) and there was a brief early mention of William Anstee, straw hat manufacturer, formerly a wool stapler of Luton. He evidently did not make such a success of his business as Mr Brown, leaving a widow with nothing but a pile of debts when he died intestate. In fact, his widow was so completely overwhelmed by the amount of debt that she issued a legal statement refusing to accept the administration of her former husband's estate, handing over all his property to his creditors to sort out between them.

In High Street North there were three more factories within a short distance of one another which were all successful in the very early 1800s, two actually next door to each other, where are now Nos. 15 and 17. On the site of the present day No. 15 was Robert Watts, who had come from Northamptonshire to set up in business here, and next to him, in what is now No. 17 (Town Hall Chambers), was William Oliver, who was also a saddler and came from a Dunstable family. And somewhere along the road was young Richard Hunter.

By the time Pigott's directory was published in 1823 there were nine straw hat manufacturers listed in Dunstable and the first of the names which would still be familiar in the late 1880s had appeared – Collings and Waterfield. Four of the other firms – Hunter's, Watts', Oliver's and Sarah Simmons' – would also still be producing hats, though the names of the owners would have changed. Hunter's would have become Elliott's, Watts' and Oliver's would be Bennett's (which would not close until 1931) and Sarah Simmons' would be Jardine's. Of the remaining three firms two were to close by 1830 and the third some twenty-odd years later, but there were also two new factories – Munt & Brown's and Blackwell's – which opened during this time.

Throughout this period the reputation of the area as the centre of the straw hat trade was growing steadily, and the 1840s saw an influx of entrepreneurs from other parts of the country, some from as far away as Scotland and the north of England. With the coming of the railway and the collapse of the coaching trade

A painting of Priory House as it was c.1812, showing the original annex on the right. The picture was painted by Thomas Fisher and now hangs in the Mayor's Parlour in Grove House. (DTC)

Priory House with the annex enlarged and converted into Munt & Brown's hat factory. The illustration is from Charles Lamborn's book Dunstaplelogia, published in 1859. (BC)

in the 1830s the town had a desperate need for a new source of employment, which the rapidly expanding industry of hat manufacturing could provide. The sale by the Burr family of their brewery and public houses in 1843 provided an opportunity for buying property which could be converted into hat factories. John Cooper, one of three Manchester brothers who were wholesalers and retailers in the drapery and related trades, bought what had been Burr's Brewery and the adjoining house and moved down here, converting the brewery into a hat factory and living in the house next door. Another new arrival was William Milligan, a Scot who came here via Dublin and set up a business with fellow Scot Alexander Forfar. For a very short period a London firm, Gregory, Cubitt & Co., took over premises which residents who lived here in the 1940s and 1950s knew as Allcorn's, in High Street North, and were followed there by another Scot, James Jardine. Richard Blackwell had established himself earlier in High Street South and his son, James, now had premises in High Street North.

As well as these newcomers arriving on the scene there were some new owners among the firms already established. Two of the early manufacturers, John Watts and Richard Hunter, had died, both leaving a young widow with a small child to bring up. Before long the two widows had re-married and their new husbands, Benjamin Bennett and William Elliott, took over the factories they had inherited from their previous partners.

Then, in 1843, one of the early manufacturers, William Oliver, died, requesting in his will that his wife should carry on the business in High Street North. But she, too, died a few years later and at some point either she or her executors rented the factory to the two Scotsmen, Messrs Forfar & Milligan. The premises were extensive, with plait rooms, workrooms, a blocking house, two steam houses, a bleach house, a 'capital' drying ground for plait, a flower garden and paved yard at the rear and a carriageway entrance from the High Street. Thirty women were employed there. Six months after Mrs Oliver's death her executors put the factory up for sale and it was bought by the man next door, Benjamin Bennett, who paid £700 and thus was able to double the size of his factory. The Forfar and Milligan partnership was soon dissolved and Mr Milligan moved along the road to the Crown, a former coaching inn previously owned by the Burrs.

As the industry expanded and the structure of the trade altered, with the suppliers of the plait coming mainly from the villages and the new buyers, the manufacturers, who were needing bigger and bigger quantities of plait, being in the town, a new group of middlemen emerged. These were the plait dealers. They bought the plait from the village women and brought it into the towns to sell to the manufacturers, setting up plait markets in the main centres of Dunstable, Luton and Hitchin, with smaller ones in several other towns and villages. The three main markets were held on different days, Luton's being on Mondays,

The house on the far right of the picture belonged originally to William Oliver and was bought by the first Benjamin Bennett in 1850. The house next to it was where Benjamin Bennett himself lived. The factory buildings were behind the houses. (DTC)

9

Hitchin's on Tuesdays and Dunstable's on Wednesdays. Individual plaiters were also free to take their plait to the markets and sell direct to the sewers and manufacturers if they wished, though the bulk of it was sold through the dealers.

Like the other markets, Dunstable found that, to avoid the market tolls and to steal a march on their competitors, dealers were beginning to trade earlier and earlier in the morning, even as early as 2.00 a.m., until eventually the Dunstable Manor Court took action and fixed the time at which trading could start at 8 o'clock in the summer and 9 o'clock in winter. The market was held in the open air, in Church Street, until 1839 when the School (now the Parish Hall) was built on the site, after which it moved to High Street North. Among the early dealers here in 1823 were John Annabel, Hannah Bloys and Henry Horn, who came from Ivinghoe Aston and who was later followed by several other members of the family.

In the mid 1800s Dunstable was growing apace. In the twenty years following 1830 the population of the town increased by about 1400, going up by 400 between 1831 and 1841 and by just over 1,000 in the next ten years. Many of the newcomers were young females who flocked to the new hat factories, and in 1851 women outnumbered the men by two to one. Many of the women came from within an area of about 25 miles radius around the town, though a few came from much further afield. The vast majority of them were bonnet sewers, most of the plaiting being done in the villages round about. There were only 153 plaiters living in Dunstable, compared with nearly 900 sewers, most of whom were probably working in the factories. This contrasts sharply with Totternhoe, for instance, where out of a total population of 753 there were 312 plaiters but only 2 bonnet sewers. Overall, there were over 10,000 females engaged in straw plaiting in Bedfordshire at the time of the 1851 census.

The number of men working in the hat trade in the town was much smaller, totalling between 70 and 80, most of them blockers, bleachers or dyers. The majority of the workers, male and female, were aged between 20 and 50 and many of them lived in lodgings. Very often their landladies were themselves plaiters or sewers, supplementing their income by taking in lodgers. Altogether at least 1,300 people, over a third of the total population, were involved with the straw trade, directly or indirectly.

The largest firms in the mid-nineteenth century were Bennett's, Blackwell's, Coopers', Elliott's, Milligan's, Munt & Brown's and Waterfield's. All of them were using old buildings originally intended for another purpose which had been converted or extended. There were by now two railway stations providing good transport links with London and the North, by way of either Leighton Buzzard or Luton, from which goods could be despatched. The straw hat manufacturing industry was well established and the town seemed set for a prosperous future.

Bonnet made at Benjamin Bennett's factory in 1835, now in Luton Museum. (LM)

Visitors to the Great Exhibition in 1851 would have seen eight stands devoted to displays by hat manufacturers. There were none from Dunstable or Luton but one, James Field & Sons from Cripplegate and Harpenden, had a big display showing how straw hats were made and the variety of plaits that could be used, including Dunstable Whole and Dunstable Patent. There was a note in the catalogue to the effect that 'At Dunstable this manufacture has long been successfully prosecuted'. Spurden, Woolley, Sanders and Co., from London, exhibited a bonnet 'made of English straw plait, showing the inner side of the straw', an innovation possibly introduced by a Dunstable manufacturer, Mr Blackwell, which produced a hat of an exceptionally attractive shade, quite different from the normal straw plait.

As the century progressed the straw hat trade here expanded rapidly, reaching its peak in the 1870s and 1880s. Round about 1850 a row of cottages in High Street North was demolished to make way for a new road to be opened up, to be called Albion Street, leading to Edward Street. This led to the establishment of a number of hat factories in this part of the town, most of them small concerns employing some 15 to 30 hands. Two exceptions were the factory of Matthew Walker, which was there for a time in the 1870s, and Warren's, there from the 1860s until it moved into High Street North in 1885/6. Both of these were on the south side of the road. Almost opposite to Warren's a London firm, Taylor Brothers, also opened a branch in the 1870s and remained there until after 1914. Among the smaller firms names which for a time were well known in the hat-making fraternity were Pickering (a name later well known in Luton), Langridge, Johnson, Squires and Mullings.

It was in the 1860s that Woolley, Sanders, as it was now called, took over the factory and high-class residence originally built by Mr James Blackwell in High Street North. Now Nos.36 to 40, it is occupied today by Oxfam, Help the Aged and the Halifax Building Society. At about the same time, or possibly slightly later, Stuart & Taylor, later Stuart & Sons, arrived in The Square.

For most of the second half of the 19th century the hat trade dominated the town and brought prosperity to the inhabitants. It provided employment for the majority of the working population and made the name of Dunstable famous for its bonnets and hats. The owners and managers of the larger firms took the lead in civic affairs and were prominent in the campaign to obtain borough status for Dunstable. And when this was achieved, they were among the first councillors, mayors and magistrates. Three of them, Mr Elliott, Mr Milligan and Mr Cooper were among the first Justices of the Peace to be appointed.

STRAW BLEACHERS.

Osborne Eliza, High st
Talbot George, High st

STRAW BONNET MANUFTRS.

Barham Jabez, High st
Bass James, High st
Bennett Benjamin, High st
Blackwell James William, High st
Blackwell Richard, High st
Budd Elizabeth, High st
Collings Thomas George, High st
Coopers John & James & George,
    High street
Elliott William, High st
Forfar & Milligan, High st
Gregory Cubitt & Co. High street, &
    Aldermanbury, *London*—(Willam
    Willis, agent)
Hawley Charlotte & Ann, High st
Henley William, West st
Henton Henry, High st
Jackson John, Houghton road
Munt & Brown, the Priory, High st,
    (and 10, Wood street, *London*—
    Samuel Collis, agent)
Osborne Eliza, High st
Rogers Josiah Thomas, High st
Waterfield Sophia, High st

List of straw hat manufacturers and straw bleachers in Dunstable from a directory of 1850.

Most of them were active in the church or chapel congregation to which they belonged. Mr Bennett, in particular, was very involved with the Methodist circuit and preached regularly in Methodist churches all round the district, sometimes at several services in different villages on the same day. John Cooper and Benjamin Bennett could always be relied upon for a donation of a good supply of hats for the Methodist church bazaars, and their wives turned up to run the stalls. At one very special bazaar to raise funds to pay off the debts on their building extensions Mr Bennett supplied a huge bonnet to be suspended over the entrance through the gateway into the Priory Field as a symbol of the town's staple industry.

Most of the factory owners and managers provided treats, as they called them, for their employees from time to time. They usually consisted of entertainments in Priory Field or the grounds of one of the larger houses, with bands, displays and plentiful supply of food. As some of the firms employed 300 to 400 workers these festivities were quite large affairs. When Coopers' held a tea at which their workers at Dunstable were joined by those from the branch factories at Houghton Regis, Toddington, Markyate and Stanbridge, 300 people sat down to the meal. It was held in Dunstable Park (the grounds of Grove House) and the 4th Bedfordshire Rifle Corps provided the music, to the 'enlivening strains' of which the guests enjoyed themselves dancing. An even bigger event must have been the Peace Celebrations at the end of the Crimean War, on 24th June 1856, when most of the hat manufacturers in the town combined to provide a memorable day for their workers and their families, and the local reporter was inspired to comment that 'we are of the opinion that everybody was well catered for'.

The owners' and managers' wives also involved themselves in their own charity work and good causes. At the outbreak of the Franco-Prussian War, in 1870, Mrs Bennett and Mrs Elliott led a group of ladies to form a branch of the National Society for Aid to the Sick and Wounded in War. Mrs Elliott did a great deal of charitable work in the town and was well known for her generosity and her 'practical piety', as her obituary has it. Mrs Cooper, though she only lived in the town for a few years before her early death in 1851, was very concerned with the welfare of the young women employed in the hat trade. The name of Mrs Hunt, wife of the manager of Munt & Brown's factory, was always to be found in the lists of contributors and helpers at local charity events.

The Dunstable Gazette of the 1870s gives a picture of a generally busy, thriving community. There was the occasional temporary slump when fashions changed faster than the industry could keep pace with – after a long period when fashions stayed relatively unaltered they began to change rapidly after 1860 – and worries about imports of foreign plait were beginning to cause concern to the

Hats made by Taylor Brothers c. 1878. (LM)

plaiters, but on the whole they were good years for the town. There were plenty of advertisements for skilled workers in the hat trade, required not only locally but also in Luton, London and St.Albans. Gregory, Cubitt & Co offered permanent employment to 100 skilled hands at their factory in Aldermanbury, in London. Suitability for some aspects of the hat trade was obviously considered a good selling point when putting property on the market and was always stressed by the auctioneers in their advertisements.

Most managers and owners of the firms lived not over the shop but in front of it, their factories having been built on to the back of the house. All the main firms except one were ultimately situated in the High Street and a number of the houses can still be seen. They were usually large and well appointed, often with a surprising amount of ground behind them, with gardens, orchards and paddocks. One hat making family, the Collings, lived in a large house (originally two) that has now become the Nationwide Building Society office and the adjoining shop (next to Barclays Bank and empty more often than not these days). The factory premises were behind the house and beyond that were extensive grounds, occupying more than two acres, including what an auctioneer referred to as a farmery, where a few livestock were kept.

Some hat manufacturers, like the Blackwells, made a fortune. When Mr Blackwell died, in 1863, his estate was valued at over £24,000 (over £1,000,000 today) and though he also owned some property in Northamptonshire much of this must have come from his hat manufacturing business. On the other hand bankruptcies were not infrequent, mostly among the small firms. But the majority of the people in the trade came somewhere in between, making an adequate or comfortable living.

The hands, as they were referred to, lived in much humbler accommodation than their employers, of course, in the terraced houses and cottages. Many of these small houses and cottages were crammed with lodgers, mainly young women employed as bonnet sewers who had moved into Dunstable from outside. The population continued to increase, from 3,589 in 1851 to 4,627 in 1881, and the proportion engaged in the straw hat trade and related occupations remained constant at about one third. Over the same period the number of houses increased enormously from just over 700 to over 1,100, the majority of them in the south-eastern part of the town, in what was known as the Borough Farm Estate, and in the area of Victoria Street, Edward Street and Matthew Street. There was a great deal of building going on and the death of one of the principal landowners in 1860 had brought a lot of building land on to the market. The British Land Company bought almost the whole of Richard Gutteridge's estate from his executors and sold it off in individual plots over the next few years.

Dunstable plait market in High Street North. From The Queen, 9th November 1861. (LM)

It was in 1867 that new legislation was passed aimed at improving conditions for all factory workers, including children, especially those in the smaller factories and workshops. Previous Factory Acts had laid down regulations governing the employment of children in the textile and coal mining industries, but not for children employed in any other kind of work. Now, for the first time, children engaged in straw plaiting were affected. According to the new Act children under the age of 8 years were not allowed to work at all and those between the ages of 9 and 13 could work part-time only if they had a certificate to prove they had attended a school (other than a plait school) for ten hours in the previous week. As many children were already plaiting by the time they were 4 or 5 the new law was obviously going to have considerable effect in this area.

The parents and the plait school mistresses argued strongly (but unsuccessfully) that, since the children did their plaiting either at home or in a plait school, and not in a factory or workshop, the new legislation should not apply to them. This was hardly surprising, of course. If the children were not allowed to work the parents would have less plait to sell and less money coming in to buy food and clothing, and the plait school mistresses, often older women, faced the prospect of losing their already small income from the fees they charged. There was also the likelihood of small children being left to wander around on their own in the daytime, with nothing to do and nowhere to go, if they were not kept busy plaiting while their parents were working.

There were several test cases over this issue, one in particular in Leighton Buzzard, but the judges ruled that whether or not the children themselves received any payment they were considered to be employed in the eyes of the law, and the intention of the Act was to prevent all children under 8 years old being made to work under any circumstances. In spite of this the law was constantly flouted. There were insufficient inspectors and those that there were often met with deception and hostility. In the end it was external factors – the passing and enforcement of the Education Act which made school attendance compulsory, together with the decline in the demand for English plait – which remedied the situation.

Working hours for women were limited to 12 hours a day, to be worked between 6a.m. and 8p.m., with meal breaks in between. Smaller firms, classed as workshops and not affected by previous legislation, had more flexibility, being allowed to fix their working hours between 6a.m. and 9p.m. Apparently the women in the factories, especially the young girls, were not generally early risers. They preferred not to start work until 9 or 9.30a.m. in the morning and then work through until 9 or 10p.m. Since both workers and employers were anxious to produce as many hats as possible in the busy season, breaches of the law were common, and one inspector for the area complained that he 'was utterly

A plaiting school. From The Queen, 9th November, 1861. (LM)

Sewing and blocking by machine and by hand. From The Illustrated London News. (LM)

disregarded' in many places. John Dony wrote that in Luton discipline in factories was unknown and employers and workers often conspired to outwit the inspectors. In the early sixties it was not uncommon for girls to work right through Friday nights at the busiest time of the year. Some cases against employers were actually brought to court and manufacturers were sometimes fined. In Dunstable Mrs Elliott, Mr Collings and Mr Bennett were all prosecuted for employing girls after the legal hours. On one occasion Mr Bennett was fined five shillings, and ordered to pay costs of eleven shillings and sixpence.

Factory girls in general were looked upon as being poorly dressed and of loose morals, but the women in the hat factories were neatly dressed and respectable, particularly those in Dunstable. They resented being thought of as factory workers and felt themselves to be a cut above those who worked in the mills in the north. Because their work was clean they could wear nice clothes and they certainly had more freedom over working hours.

During this period there was also some further legislation aimed at improving the workers' lot. In December 1869 the Gazette published an announcement of a new law to reduce overcrowding in the workplace; in future the amount of space allocated to each person in the workroom was to be fixed at 500 cubic feet. And in the 1870s four annual bank holidays were introduced, on Easter Monday, Whit Monday, the first Monday in August and Boxing Day.

As the number of hat making firms grew it was natural that the manufacturers should unite to promote their common interests. By the early 1850s a problem which they all found themselves facing was that of dishonest trading in the straw plait business. Plait was always bought and sold in bundles called 'scores', nominally twenty yards long. But more and more frequently the scores were found to be considerably less than 20 yards, sometimes as little as 16 yards in length. A public meeting of those involved in the trade was organised in Luton in March 1852 and the Straw Hat Manufacturers Association was formed to try and deal with the problem. A committee of nine men was elected, among them three representatives from Dunstable – Mr John Cooper, Mr William Elliott and Mr Samuel Collis (manager of Munt and Brown's Dunstable factory). Member firms paid an annual subscription of 2s. 6d. and an inspector was appointed to go round the markets checking the scores. Plait dealers were asked to attach a label to each bundle with the words 'Warranted 20 Yards to the Score' printed on it. But the problem obviously persisted for many years. William Austin, from Luton, reported that 2,538 cases of short measure were recorded even as late as 1868. Eventually the problem seems to have resolved itself when most of the plait was imported and straw plaiting locally died out.

The opening of two covered-in plait halls in Luton in 1869 sparked off a

THE
STRAW HAT MANUFACTURERS
ASSOCIATION,

ESTABLISHED TO PREVENT
Short Measure in Plait,

Announces to the Trade that a Public Meeting was held at the Town Hall, Luton, on Monday, the 8th of March, 1852,

MR. JAMES WALLER, IN THE CHAIR.

WHEN THE FOLLOWING

RESOLUTIONS

WERE UNANIMOUSLY ADOPTED.

The 1st.   Moved by Mr. JAMES MUIR, seconded by Mr. ALFRED TANSLEY, and supported by Mr. FERRABY,

"That a Society be formed, for the purpose of securing FULL MEASURE in all Straw Plaiting, Trimmings, &c. to be called *The Straw Hat Manufacturers Association*. That it be managed by a Committee of nine Manufacturers resident in the District, and that the Members of the Association pledge themselves generally to support and co-operate with the Committee in order to suppress this evil of the trade."

The 2nd.   Moved by Mr. WILLIAM BOLTON, seconded by Mr. ROBERT HOW, and supported by Mr. ALFRED WELCH,

"That all Manufacturers Subscribing annually Two Shillings and Sixpence and upwards be Members of the Society. That the Fund so raised be at the disposal of the Committee for the time being, who shall be authorized to engage a paid Agent to attend the Plait Markets for the Inspection of the Plait. That he report thereon, and act as the Committee shall from time to time direct."

The 3rd.   Moved by Mr. SAMUEL COLLIS, seconded by Mr. CHARLES WALLER, and supported by Mr. HIGGINS,

"That all Dealers attending the Plait Markets be requested to attach to the bundles of plait sold, a *Ticket* with the words *Warranted 20 Yards to the Score*, printed on it. That the Society recommend its Members to encourage as far as possible only those persons who are connected with the Plait Dealers Association."

The 4th.   Moved by Mr. GUSTAVUS JORDAN, and seconded by Mr. SAMUEL GRUNDY,

"That the following Gentlemen be appointed a Committee for the Year 1852, viz: Messrs. JAMES WALLER, CHARLES WALLER, W. H. HIGGINS, WILLIAM BOLTON, ALFRED WELCH, and JAMES MUIR; for Luton; Messrs. JOHN COOPER, W. ELLIOTT, and SAMUEL COLLIS, for Dunstable. That a GENERAL MEETING of the Members be held in the month of December next, or at such time as the Committee may think necessary, to report proceedings for the consideration of such business connected with the movement as may be brought before the Meeting, and for the election of a new Committee."

In giving further publicity to the foregoing Resolutions, the Committee urge the Support of ALL Parties concerned, that an effectual check may be given at once to the evil so bitterly and justly complained of.

WISEMAN, PRINTER, LUTON.

Notice of resolutions to be put to a meeting of straw hat manufactures to deal with the problem of short measure in the plait market. (LM)

campaign to have a permanent indoor plait hall built in Dunstable. A speaker at an Odd Fellows' Dinner in 1871 first mooted the idea, estimating that the cost would be £2,500. The Town Council however, had other ideas. Though they agreed in principle with replacing the open-air market with a covered-in plait hall, they had another suggestion as to how it should be done.

When, in 1864, Dunstable had been granted a charter giving it borough status, one of the new Town Council's first actions had been to buy the old Market House as a municipal building. Though they had added a clock tower in 1869, two years later they were still discussing how to make the best use of the building. One of the Councillors, Mr Limbrey, now came up with a scheme to use part of it for a plait hall. He pointed out, as an inducement to persuade councillors to vote for the scheme, that the Plait Hall at Luton was 'a very profitable speculation'.

Hearing of this proposal Mr Henry Elliott, one of the sons of the Elliott hat manufacturing family, who was by then a professional architect with a London practice, wrote to offer his services for the project. (It is not stated whether this as to be a gift to his native town or on a professional basis.) His offer was accepted and after several more months of deliberation the Council decided that most of the lower floor of the building would be used as a plait hall. In September 1872 W.H. Derbyshire wrote that there were plans to convert 'the unattractive and inconvenient buildings into an imposing structure, containing a Magistrates' Court, Plait Hall and Corn Exchange' in the following year and in the autumn of 1874 there was a grand opening ceremony of the splendidly refurbished building.

Unfortunately, some five years later, in December 1879, there was a devastating fire, and they had to start all over again. Once the insurance claim was sorted out the Town Council moved rather faster on this occasion, and the following January Mr Elliott came to a Council meeting to present his proposed plans for the new building.

The good news was that the façade of the old building had survived the fire and remained sound, apart from a part of the parapet, which could easily be repaired. The restored building would be surmounted by a new clock tower, approximately the same size as the previous one, which would have 'a very nice appearance indeed, being more in accordance with the character of the building than the last'. The plait hall and the corn exchange were to be one great room, 'separated and distinct from the Town Hall above', with a separate entrance. There was to be 'a contrivance' (not described) between the ceiling of this and the floor above to deaden the sound. Mr Bennett agreed to sell a small plot of land to the rear of the Crown to provide the extra ground needed for Mr Elliott's scheme. The plan was immediately accepted by the Council and the work was

The old Town Hall, largely destroyed by fire in December 1879. (DG)

put out to tender. To Dunstablians who remember the builders Robinson & White it is interesting to note that among the tenders received was one from Mr Joseph Robinson and one from Mr Frederick White. The contract was actually awarded to Mr Frederick White for the sum of £1,690.0.0, which was £500 less than Mr Robinson's quotation. Work was to start on 1st March 1880 and be finished in six months, with a penalty clause imposing a fine of £10 per week if the work was not completed on time. So once again there was a grand opening attended by all the great and the good of the town.

The main plait dealers in Dunstable then were the members of the Horn family. The first to arrive here was Henry, who came from Ivinghoe Aston some time before 1823 and had premises first in West Street and later in High Street South. His son, Cornelius, followed him into the trade, at first in Edward Street and later in Victoria Street. Four more members of the family followed later, nephews of Henry and sons of his brother Francis. The first of them was Eli who came from Ivinghoe Aston as a young man in about 1852 and obviously was very successful in the business. He was still comparatively young when he died about twenty years later but even so he was sufficiently well off to leave £1,000 to each of his three children. The house he had planned for himself in Albion Street, which later came to be known as Albion Villa, was still in the course of construction at the time of his death, but his widow, Sarah, moved in when it was completed and lived there for the remainder of her life. Eli was elected as a Town Councillor in 1869 and quite probably would have become mayor at some point had he lived longer. He had three brothers, Francis, George and Reuben, all of whom became plait dealers. Like his brother, Francis appears to have been very successful in business and his descendants are still in the hat trade. He lived at one time in a very substantial house in High Street South, later known as Glenlossie, with a warehouse adjoining, next door to Mr Blackwell's house and factory. (Both were demolished to make way for Viceroy Court.)

George Horn lived for a time in the Grey House (the Downtown Café), which afterwards became Eliza Osborne's hat factory, but when he was declared bankrupt in 1870 he moved to St. Mary's Street. About Reuben little is known apart from his marriage to Jane Wood at Little Gaddesden in 1869 and the fact that he lived in Princes Street.

It was in 1870 that the straw hat manufacturers of Luton and Dunstable made common cause once again, though this time the partnership was not to end so harmoniously. The Second Reform Bill introduced three years earlier by Disraeli had proposed the redistribution of the seats in the House of Commons, giving parliamentary representation to some of the industrial areas for the first time. In the first draft of the Bill Luton was included as one of the towns to be enfranchised, but during its passage through the Commons Luton was removed from the list in favour of another town. The manufacturers of Luton felt strongly that, since those employed in the textile trades, the iron works and even the shoemaking industry in Northampton were represented in Parliament, those engaged in the straw hat trade should be treated in the same way. What was more, the population of Luton, Dunstable and District was 40,000 and many towns with an MP to represent them had much smaller populations, some only 5,000. The MPs for Bedfordshire, though worthy men, represented the agricultural interests of the county. A deputation from Luton approached Colonel Gilpin, M.P., of Hockliffe, seeking his support and advice. He promised his support and suggested that they should invite Dunstable to join them in submitting a Petition to Parliament, which he felt would strengthen their case. Accordingly Dunstable Council were invited to a public meeting in Luton and the invitation was accepted.

The meeting took place on 13th June 1870. After outlining the background to the situation Mr William Bigg, the Chairman, invited comments from the floor. At the appropriate time he put to the meeting the resolution 'That in the opinion of this meeting the towns of Luton and Dunstable, with the district, are entitled to Representation in the Commons House of Parliament'. Hands were already going up in favour when a Mr Gilder called out that he had something to say. He was invited on to the platform to speak and said he opposed including Dunstable. In his view Luton was more likely to succeed on its own, it would be less expensive to go it alone and there would be 'less jealousies'. (There were cries of 'No! No! 'from the audience). The seconder of the amendment added that he felt that Luton would have no chance of gaining representation if they were joined with Dunstable. The amendment to exclude Dunstable was then put to the meeting and passed by a large majority. At this, one of the Dunstable Councillors, Mr W H Derbyshire, rose and said that, as their presence at the meeting was no longer necessary they would withdraw, but reserved the right to take whatever action they felt necessary on their own account. The Chairman thanked the Dunstable delegation for coming and the Dunstable Councillors made a dignified departure. The result of this was that both towns applied independently to be represented in Parliament, but neither town was successful and it was many years before Luton had an MP of its own. The episode, however, brought some notoriety to the area. The meeting was reported in the London paper Figaro, and there was some lively correspondence in the local papers for the next week or two.

As in all industries there was a steady shift towards mechanisation in straw hat manufacturing in the 19th century, the Victorians being nothing if not inventive. But in spite of all the technical progress there was one process that always had to be done by hand – the plaiting of the straw in the first instance. After the invention of the splitter the method of plaiting remained unaltered, although there were one or two unsuccessful attempts to invent a machine to do the work, but no mechanical device could ever replace the nimble-fingered plaiters. There was, however, no such problem with the other processes and the methods used for bleaching, dyeing, sewing and blocking all changed over time.

In the early days bleaching had been done by the plaiters themselves by placing the straw or finished plait in a box of molten sulphur. Dyeing was done with vegetable dyes (not, as local legend has it, with plums!), but dyeing finished plait was always difficult. It was easier, if colour was required, to dye the straw first and make it up into a multi-coloured plait. When aniline dyes were introduced in the 1850s dyeing and bleaching became specialised fields and in Luton the two processes were usually carried out together in separate premises, away from the factory. In Dunstable, however, the hat factories usually had their own bleaching room and only relied on outside sources for the dyeing process. From soon after the time when aniline dyes were introduced several bleachers and dyers went into business on their own account in Dunstable and in 1885 there were four dyers listed in the town – Henry Henton in Victoria Street, William Axtell in Union Street (in business since 1861), John De'Long in the Square and James Holt in West Street, although in fact the directory was out of date and Mr Holt had died the previous year. His had been the largest dye works in the town, employing 18 men and 3 boys. After his death the premises were sold and the auctioneer's catalogue described them as consisting of a boiler house with a chimney shaft 70 feet high, fitted with a Cornish boiler and a donkey pump, a dyehouse, a warehouse, cutting and drying rooms, storehouses and other buildings. These and the adjoining house, Ebenezer Villa, were bought by Arthur White for £745 and ceased to be used as a dye works. So far their exact location has not been identified.

Once the sewing machine had been invented in America it was only a matter of time before somebody adapted it for use in the straw hat trade. Treadle sewing machines came into use in the trade in the 1870s and one of the best-known manufacturers was Wilcox and Gibbs. In Dunstable Matthew Walker had 16 machines for sewing hats, which were said to do the work of six or seven people very efficiently and he actually patented what was known as a concealed-stitch machine in the early 1880s. Vyse and Son in Luton had 15 sewing machines on which 15 workers could produce the same number of hats as 50 hand sewers in the same time. Workers at home could hire a machine for three shillings a week and one could be bought for £3.10.0. In 1881 there were nearly 700 women in Dunstable sewing hats, some by machine and some by hand. Compared with

Alderman W. H. Derbyshire, one of the delegation who went to Luton to discuss a joint petition for Parliamentary representation for Luton and Dunstable. (DTC)

1851 the figures showed a drop in numbers of about 200, which was probably largely due to the introduction of machines. Looking at the census returns it is not possible to be sure how many women were working in the factories and how many at home. Judging by the numbers of workers employed by the large factories like Coopers' and Munt & Brown's it seems likely that the majority of them were working in the factories.

After sewing, straw hats needed to be stiffened before being blocked to give them their shape. Stiffening was done by immersing the hats in gelatine or some similar substance, draining off the excess solution and hanging them up to dry. An advertisement in 1859 'respectfully invited' hat manufacturers to try Nutting's Snow White Granules as a 'superior stiffener' for bonnets. They cost sixpence a packet from the local chemist, but there was no indication as to what they consisted of. Shellac dissolved in spirit was also sometimes used later.

Blocking, like dyeing and bleaching, was done by men. Early blocks were made of wood and blockmaking was in itself a skilled trade. As fashions changed a new block would be needed for each new style and the blockmakers would produce them to order, in their own workshops. There were several blockmakers in Dunstable from 1850 onwards, though most did not stay in the trade for long. There was just one whose name appeared in the directories for nearly 30 years, Thomas Cheshire, first in Union Street and then in Matthew Street. When all-metal blocking machines came into use in the 1870s there was, of course, less demand for the blockmaker's skill, the wooden blocks only being needed to produce a mould from which the metal shape could be cast.

In the early days blocking was done by placing the stiffened hat on the wooden block, steaming it to soften it and then pressing it into shape with a glass slicken stone, as it was called, shaped like a bun or a mushroom. The first machines to be invented were made of wood and hand operated; later ones were made of metal and eventually hydraulically operated. Blocking rooms were generally part of the Dunstable factories, though two independent blockers were still advertising in 1885 and a blocking machine was advertised for as little as £6.0.0 in the Hatters' Gazette in 1873. As early as 1869 an advertisement had appeared in the Dunstable Gazette for Herresford's Blocking Machine which could only be obtained from 'the sole agent, Frederick Sanders, at Messrs J & G Coopers'. Customers were invited to inspect the machine at Messrs Coopers' factory.

New machines were being patented all the time, and existing ones improved. It was all a far cry from the days when the women would make a few hats at home and take them to sell to the stage-coach travellers outside the Sugar Loaf. In 1880 the women worked in factories producing hats by the thousand, which were sold all over the world.

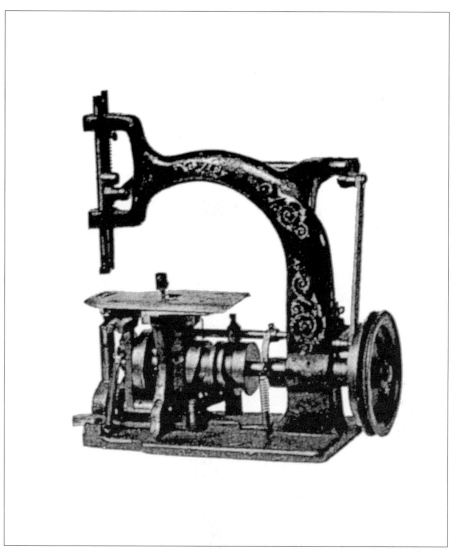

A concealed-stitch hat sewing machine patented by Mathew Walker, a Dunstable hat manufacturer. (LM)

Machines had helped to keep the straw hat manufacturing business competitive and the manufacturing industry was doing well in the early 1880s. Unfortunately it was a different story for the straw plaiters who were unable to compete with the foreign competition when plait from China, known as Canton, began to be imported in the 1870s. It was the familiar story of cheap labour in the Far East being exploited to undercut prices, resulting in the home industry gradually being reduced and finally forced out of existence. Although Canton plait was admitted to be inferior to the English it was considered adequate for most of the industry's needs and far less expensive. From then on the market for English plait steadily declined and by the end of the century the craft of plaiting was almost extinct in this area.

There was some attempt to revive it in the 1890s and as part of the campaign the Technical Instruction Committee of Bedfordshire County Council held an exhibition in Luton of the work of pupils attending plaiting classes in Bedfordshire and Buckinghamshire. As well as plait for hats there were examples of other articles ingeniously made of straw – baskets, mats, slippers, dolls' cradles and furniture, etc. Mr Simon Whitbread, M.P., speaking at the exhibition, was of the opinion that the industry should be encouraged and said he would like to see it as a cottage industry again. But it was a hopeless battle. Another speaker reported that the amount of plait being imported was going up dramatically year by year. Realistically he felt that 'No hope of competing under present circumstances with either China or Japan can be entertained', though he thought that there was some chance of competing successfully with Italy and Switzerland, from which much smaller quantities of good quality plait were imported.

By this time, though, it was not only the plaiting industry that was in difficulties. The whole of the straw hat manufacturing trade was also having to compete with a huge tide of foreign imports and there were warnings that everyone would be in the same situation as the plaiters in a few years' time if the imports continued at the same rate. To make matters worse the demand for straw hats in this country was declining as fashions changed and felt hats became more popular.

In Dunstable the effects of these problems were already evident. By 1900 all the smaller firms in Albion Street had gone and some of the High Street firms had closed, too. Where there had been family firms the sons had not carried on the businesses of their fathers. Some firms with factories in Luton as well as Dunstable moved all their operations to their Luton works. Shortly after Mrs Elliott's death her son, by then in his sixties, had retired and closed the factory in High Street North. The last of the Waterfields retired in the 1890s and the

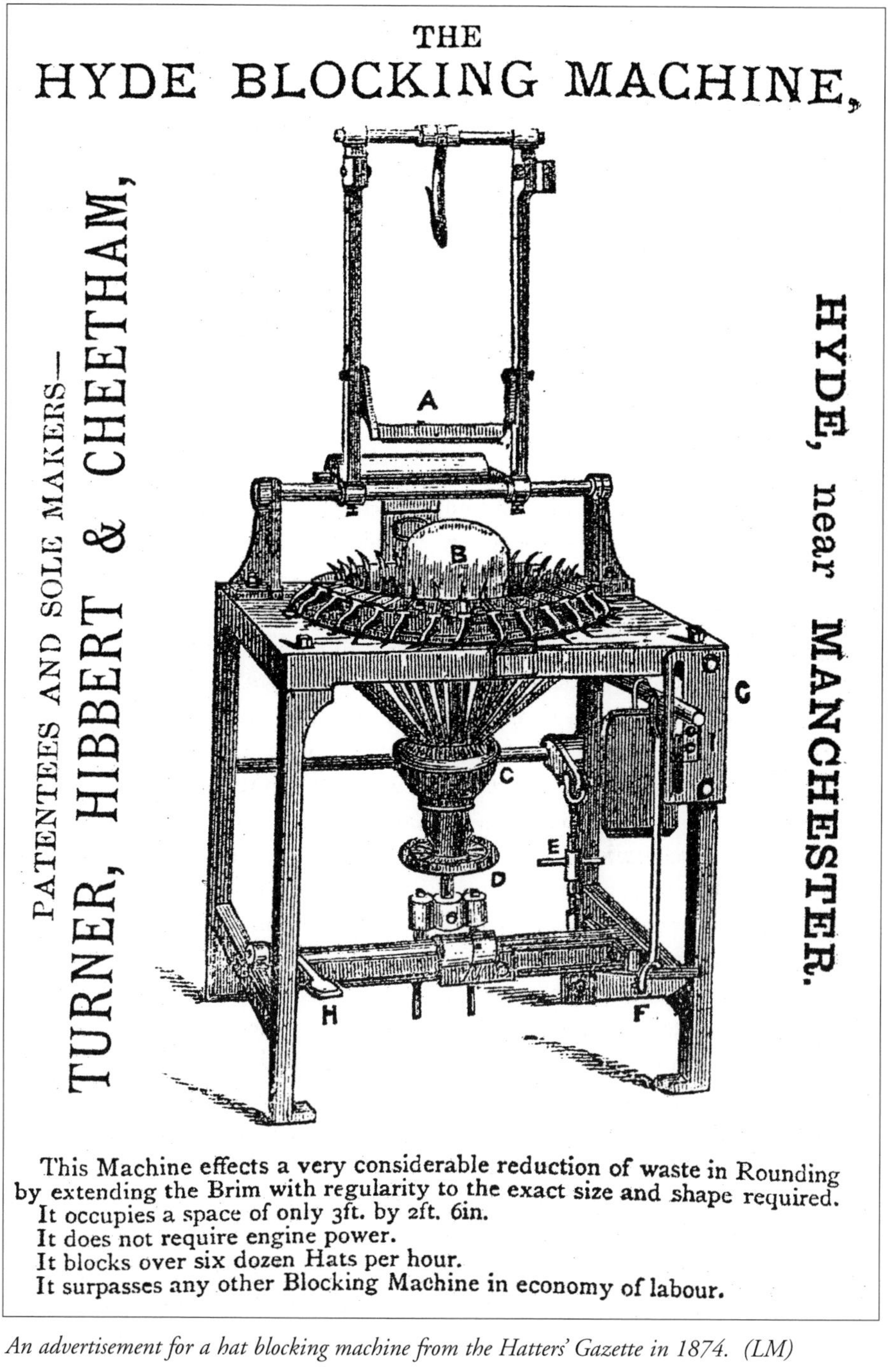

THE
HYDE BLOCKING MACHINE,

PATENTEES AND SOLE MAKERS—

TURNER, HIBBERT & CHEETHAM

HYDE, near MANCHESTER.

A

B

C

C

D

E

H

F

This Machine effects a very considerable reduction of waste in Rounding by extending the Brim with regularity to the exact size and shape required.
It occupies a space of only 3ft. by 2ft. 6in.
It does not require engine power.
It blocks over six dozen Hats per hour.
It surpasses any other Blocking Machine in economy of labour.

An advertisement for a hat blocking machine from the Hatters' Gazette in 1874. (LM)

family business came to an end after nearly one hundred years. Mr Cooper had retired to Manchester some years before and the factory had closed in about 1878 and stood empty for many years. Montague Collings had moved to Luton, Jardine's and Eliza Osborne's had closed. Dunstable bonnets had been famous for their quality, 'a hall-mark of fashionable elegance', and Dunstable had been regarded as 'the natural home of the hat and bonnet industry', to quote the Luton News. But times and fashions had changed.

Back in the 1870s some far-sighted manufacturers in Luton had already begun to produce felt hats. They bought the basic 'forms', or 'hoods', ready made from factories in the north of England and dyed and blocked them to produce finished hats. Work in the felt trade was useful because it provided employment in the periods when the straw trade was slack, and this side of the hat industry was gradually expanded in Luton until the town had a monopoly of the trade in the years before the Second World War. The larger Dunstable hat firms also produced some felts and velours, but never on the same scale as the Luton firms, perhaps because the machinery was very expensive and it was an investment the small firms could not afford, and the larger firms, with factories in Luton, found it more economic to concentrate all their production in one place.

Prospects for the trade as the new century began were distinctly gloomy, so there must have been some alarm in Dunstable when the premises occupied by Stuart & Sons, in the Square, were put up for auction after the death of the owner. The executors of the Rev. Thomas Gostelow Lockhart put a reserve price on the property when it came up for sale at the beginning of 1907, but the bidding only reached £1,950 and it was withdrawn. Stuart & Sons continued to occupy the factory and the workers' jobs were, for the moment, secure. The factory continued to operate for another eighteen years and finally closed in 1925.

The workers in the factory across the road were not so fortunate. The town was stunned when, without warning, news came of the collapse of Munt & Brown in the summer of 1908. The company had been burdened for years with the task of trying to recover debts owing to it over a very long period and there was only one member of either family still actively engaged in its management, Harry Brown, then aged 72. After a long struggle against the odds to keep the firm going he had finally had to give up and been forced to call a meeting of his creditors. The firm's factories in London, Dunstable and St. Albans were immediately closed. Several months afterwards Mr Arthur Munt, a son of one of the original founders of the company, came to live at Priory House and had the factory next door demolished, allowing a view of the Priory Church from the High Street 'for the first time in modern history', as a Gazette reporter wrote. This the writer apparently considered to be 'some consolation', presumably for

Advertisement for a trade exhibition of straw plait and straw hats held in Luton in 1885 in an attempt to boost the industry. (LM)

the unemployment caused, though it must have been small consolation to those who had lost their livelihoods.

In the spring following the closure of Munt & Brown's there was some attempt to boost the straw hat trade and a writer in a London daily paper was predicting that 'given a fine Easter, there will be a revival of the Dunstable bonnet, which grew so popular with the ladies of the early Victorian era. About ten years ago this bonnet was quite the vogue, but no version could be prettier than a genuine revival of the bonnet of half a century ago'. Whether or not the Easter was fine the prediction was not fulfilled and a few years later the trade was in desperate straits. By 1914 it was said to be impossible to make a profit from the manufacture of straw hats.

A new enterprise at about this time was the factory built by Mr Sydney Aylott in Luton Road, just beyond the railway arch, on the northern side of the road. Mr Aylott had had a hat factory in Cheapside, in Luton, but the one in Dunstable was different. On one slope of its roof, painted in large letters, was proclaimed the name of Mr Aylott's new company, The Dunstable Hat Renovating Company Ltd. There hats were cleaned, sometimes re-blocked, and generally re-furbished, and some hats may actually have been made there. It operated for a number of years, the original premises being extended more than once, the last time being in 1922 when a temporary steaming room was added. The works closed in the mid-twenties, the Renovating Company moved to West Parade and the Luton Road building was occupied for a few years by Messrs Parrott & Jackson. Ogden & Cleaver, builders' merchants, followed them and after their departure the premises became the depot for a large dairy. Today McDonald's stands on the site.

In the 1920s there was a general exodus from the town of the last remaining firms. Taylor Brothers left Albion Street in about 1915 and Stuart & Sons closed in 1925. Woolley, Sanders transferred its operations to its Luton factory in 1927 and sold off its Dunstable premises. At the end of 1928 Mr Warren announced that he was moving all his work to his factory in Bute Street in Luton, which meant the end of the last full-scale hat manufacturing operations in Dunstable. Bennett's was already cutting down on the amount of work carried out in the High Street North premises and ceased production here completely in 1931.

Most of the premises formerly used for the hat trade which had frontages on the High Street were converted into shops on the ground floor. Waterfield's, next to the Sugar Loaf, had already become Durrant's before 1900. A few doors away Woolley, Sanders' became the Cycle & Wireless shop, the Whipsiderry Café and the Central Café. Jardine's became the office of the estate agent, Mr Thorpe, and was demolished to make way for the Quadrant shopping precinct in the 1960s.

The Dunstable Hat Renovating Company's factory in Luton Road. McDonald's stands on the site today. (DG)

THE
DUNSTABLE
HAT RENOVATING LTD
COMPANY

Part of Mr Collings' premises became first the London & County Bank, then a post office and later a cinema before becoming a shop. The other part was for many years Charlie Cole's cycle shop, with its famous penny-farthing bicycle suspended above the door, and is today occupied by the Nationwide Building Society. Bennett's (Town Hall Chambers), Elliott's and Warren's all became shops. In High Street South, fortunately, Priory House and Norton House still survive, the latter once the home of the manager of Stuart & Sons and now used as offices, and Eliza Osborne's factory is now the Downtown Café.

A few small workshops remained in the town where some outwork was done for the Luton factories, chiefly sewing and trimming. Up until 1900 hats had been sent out by the manufacturers without any trimmings. These were added by the milliners, some of them in independent shops, others in a special department in a big store, where the well-off could have the trimmings done to their own requirements. Women who could not afford such luxuries trimmed their own hats and changed the ribbons and other adornments as and when fashion required. From about 1900 onwards the manufacturers began to sell their hats ready trimmed, some of the work being done within the factory and some by outworkers.

One workshop doing this kind of work in Dunstable was run by Miss Julia Potter and was situated in the Maypole Yard, off West Street. (It was sometimes referred to by local people as a hat factory.) Miss Potter rented the premises from the Bennett Estate and ran the business at least into the 1940s. The building is still there, on the right-hand side just inside the entrance to the yard from West Street.

Two other trades associated with hat making still survived in Dunstable in the twentieth century. One of these was blockmaking. In Burr Street there was a workshop and yard belonging to the Dolmans, some of whom were carpenters and builders and some blockmakers. The first blockmaker in the family to be mentioned was William, who was in business in St Mary's Street in 1891, where his father had had a small works making polishing cloths. In the early years of the 20th century he had moved to Burr Street and in the inter-war period five Dolman brothers were working there as blockmakers, sharing the yard and workshops with other members of the family who were builders and carpenters. The blockmakers worked at this time for a Luton factory, collecting the new style hats from them and returning the finished blocks. The firm of Dolmans finally closed in 1978, though the blockmaking is believed to have finished earlier. A small housing development has now been built on the site of the yard and is to be named Dolman's Place. One other blockmaker still working in Dunstable until well into the 20th century was John Bandy (or Bundy), of King Street.

The second trade was the making of cardboard boxes. The hat trade used thousands of these to transport their hats by rail and road and so began this

The Dolman family and other blockmakers at Dolman's Yard in about 1930. L. to R. Len Stokes, Albert Dolman, William (Bill) Dolman, Harold Abrahams, Arthur Dolman, John Dolman, Hedley Coombs, Ezra Cook. (MD)

subsidiary industry. The biggest firm in Dunstable was Parrott and Jackson's, who started in Manchester Place in the early 1920s. It was they who took over the factory vacated by the Dunstable Hat Renovating Company in Luton Road sometime between 1924 and 1928, and from there they moved three more times, each time moving further along the road towards Luton. Even when they started there was very little hat manufacturing still being done here and their trade was always with the Luton companies. As the hat trade declined so, of course, did the demand for hat boxes, and in the latter years the firm made boxes for a variety of purposes. The family finally sold out in the late 1980s. A much smaller concern was that of Alan Weatherill, who took out a lease in 1938 for seven years for the former bleach room, blocking room and boiler room at 17 High Street North, for the production of cardboard boxes.

The end of the straw hat industry in Dunstable must inevitably have meant much hardship and unemployment. Some of the women went to work in the Luton factories, or worked from home, while for men there were openings at Waterlow's printing works and at Harrison Carter's, where they made heavy industrial equipment. Both of these firms had arrived in the 1890s, but there was no large-scale employment for women until the arrival of Cross Paperware in 1909. Today it is often forgotten what a thriving hat trade Dunstable once had, but for 50 years it had been its staple industry and brought prosperity to the town.

PART II

FAMILIES, FIRMS AND FACTORIES

Up until 1960 most of the buildings connected with the hat industry in Dunstable were still standing; only Coopers' and Munt & Brown's factories had been completely demolished. In the sweeping changes which took place in Dunstable in the next two decades almost all the factories which lay behind the High Street houses, and some of the buildings actually on the High Street, were knocked down to make way for the new shopping precincts. In spite of this a surprising number still remain, though they are not always instantly recognisable to the casual passer-by.

The hat trail starts at the cross roads, outside the Nag's Head, proceeds along High Street North as far as Cubes Night Club and back up the other side of the road, across to High Street South and along as far as the Downtown Café, returning back down the other side of the road to The Square. It takes in most of the original buildings which still survive today and some which have replaced the ones that have gone.

But an industry is not just buildings. It is the stories of the people behind it that bring it to life. While it has been possible to find out a great deal about the background of some of the local family firms, very little has been found about some of the London companies' branches. Some of the accounts that follow are therefore quite long, others are very brief, but they all contribute in some measure to the story of Dunstable's hat industry.

A few doors along from the Nag's Head are Nos. 15 and 17 High Street North. No. 15 is a late 19th century house built on the site of the first Mr Bennett's original house, with shop fronts on the ground floor today. No. 17 is an 18th century building which was once William Oliver's factory and the large front window to the right on the ground floor, curved at the top, is fitted into the archway which was the entrance to the carriageway through from the High Street to the yard at the rear.

At the time when Benjamin Bennett first came to Dunstable as a young man John Watts was living in the house next to William Oliver's factory. (The Anchor inn, now the White Horse, was on the other side of it.) There his father, Robert Watts, had started a straw hat factory in about 1800 which John had taken over on his father's death.

The young Benjamin had come from Aspley Guise and started his career in the town as a beer retailer, following one of his father's occupations (the other was farming). Brought up as a staunch Methodist he soon joined the local congregation and was one of the trustees of the first Methodist Chapel when it was built in 1831, even though he had only been in the town a year or so. So far there had been no hint of his having any interest in the hat trade. He may already have known the young Mr & Mrs Watts when John died at the early age of 32, or he may have become acquainted with Sarah after her husband's death. At all events he and Sarah Watts were married in 1835, she being nine years older than he. As a widow she had inherited her husband's property, so when she married Benjamin Bennett he found himself the owner of a hat factory. From then on he concentrated on the hat trade and eventually gave up all connection with the brewing business.

Benjamin and Sarah had three sons who grew up to adulthood, Benjamin, Robert and John, and Sarah's son by her first marriage, Henry, grew up alongside them. Business prospered and in 1850, when the factory next door came up for sale after William Oliver and his wife had died, Mr Bennett bought it for £700. Initially it was rented out to the two young Scotsmen, Alexander Forfar and William Milligan, but very soon they moved out and Mr Bennett combined the newly acquired premises with his existing factory, making it one of the largest privately owned firms in the town, employing nearly 100 workers in the 1870s. And over the course of time he added an extensive range of buildings to the rear of the original factories.

Mr Bennett was, by all accounts, one of those people who became a 'character' known to everybody around the town. As a leading Methodist lay preacher he had what was described as a voice of thunder, and his speaking

PARTICULARS.

LOT 1,

Comprises a well-built, 10-Roomed, Sash Fronted, Brick, Timber, and Slated

DWELLING-HOUSE,

SITUATE IN HIGH STREET,

Including the extensive Plait and Work-Rooms, Blocking House, Two Steam Houses, Bleach House, with a large Tank and Lead Pump to same, Stable, Capital Drying Ground for Plait, surrounded by a substantial Brick Wall, Flower Garden, Paved Yard, with a Carriage-Way Entrance from the front Street to the rear of the Premises, and a beautiful Well of Water, late in the occupation of MRS. WILLIAM OLIVER, deceased, who has carried on a most extensive Business as a Straw Hat Manufacturer for many years.

For a view of the Estate, apply to Mr. Henton, High Street, Dunstable, and the Auctioneer.

Description of 17 High Street North from the auctioneer's sale catalogue in 1850. (BLARS)

'abounded in anecdotes and illustrations'. Physically he was a strong man; he was astute in business and generous by nature. Many a bazaar or fund-raising event benefited from his generosity.

His faith was extremely important to him and he would sometimes invite a preacher to come into his factory and address the workers. One Sunday in 1865, when he was still only 56, he was taking his fifth service of the day when he had a severe stroke. He was not expected to survive but he pulled through, although he had to teach himself to talk again and he remained partially paralysed for the rest of his life. In spite of his disabilities he always remained cheerful, enjoying his regular morning walks and rides and his visits to friends.

The running of the business was taken over by his eldest son, Benjamin, who had qualified as a lawyer and been called to the Bar, but never practised. Instead he became a very successful business man and built up the Bennett empire, opening a second hat factory in Luton and going into the brewing business, the trade in which his father had started his career. He leased a brewery in Harpenden and in 1887 acquired the North-Western Brewery in Dunstable, previously owned by Green & Cutler (formerly Henchman & Cutler), which became known familiarly in the town as Bennett's Brewery. He was very much

43

involved in civic affairs, became a Town Councillor and a County Councillor and Mayor of Dunstable in 1871.

No doubt the family fortunes were enhanced when he married into a wealthy local family, the Anstees. His bride was Miss Mary Anstee, who was the daughter of Charlotte and John Anstee of Lewsey. After their marriage the couple lived first in a house almost opposite to Benjamin Bennett Senior's, in High Street North; from there they moved to The Cheveralls in Flamstead and thence to Kensworth House. Both were great supporters of St Mary's Church in Kensworth and of the village school, and though the younger Benjamin was not a Methodist, like his father, he also supported the Methodist church in the village. (Both of his brothers were ordained as clergymen in the Church of England.) Over the years he steadily extended the Bennett Estate and acquired a great deal of property in Kensworth and Dunstable.

Benjamin Bennett Senior lived on for another 17 years after his stroke and died where he had lived, in the house next door to the Anchor. His wife, to whom he said he owed all his success and whose advice he always relied upon, had died some years earlier. His stepson, Henry Watts, never married and stayed with him to the end of his life.

Mr Bennett's obituary, which appeared in the Dunstable Gazette of 13th December 1882, must have been one of the longest ever to appear in the paper and the description of his funeral is tremendously detailed. The funeral car (as it was called) was 'universally admired', it being the first time one like it had been seen in the county. It was not black, as we might have expected, being accustomed to the sombre black hearse used today, but 'painted crimson lake, relieved with gold' and 'furnished with drapery to correspond'.

Henry Watts remained in the house in High Street North until his death in 1891. The following year Benjamin Bennett had a new house built on the site, which is the building that stands there today, currently (2003) a house agent's office. For many years it was occupied by Thomas Weatherill, a manager at Bennett's, who named it Garraby after the village in Yorkshire from which his family had come and whose descendants continued to live there until the 1940s. No. 17, now called Town Hall Chambers, was divided into two and one side became the Bennett Estate office, the other being used as part of the hat factory.

The Estate continued to prosper under the direction of the younger Benjamin, who was probably better known in the end for his brewing enterprises than as a hat manufacturer. He died in 1911 leaving an estate in excess of £153,000. There were no children to succeed him and he left a will so complicated that there were many occasions when the people concerned had to resort to a court of law to try to determine how it should be interpreted. At one hearing in the Chancery

44

Benjamin Bennett the Younger. He served as Mayor of Dunstable 1871-2. (DTC)

Division the judge, Mr Justice Eve, is said to have described it as one of the most difficult he had ever come across, because it was 'so long, verbose, and, in some respects, so conflicting'. In that particular case there were no less than eight parties involved, each with their own King's Counsel representing them.

In general terms the will provided that his widow, Mary, should have the use of their London residence, in Stanhope Gate, for the rest of her life, with an income to be paid out of the estate. After some smaller bequests he left the bulk of his estate, with certain conditions, to be held in trust for twenty years for two nieces, Louisa Charlotte Susannah Anstee and Amy Cecil Mary Bennett, with the stipulation that the beneficiary not bearing the name of Bennett should 'assume the same by Royal Licence'. When Louisa later married Mr Stanley Jones it was not she, therefore, who changed her name to his, but he who changed his name to hers and he became known as Stanley Bennett. Amy Bennett never married. The estate was not left to be equally divided between the two nieces; the property that each was to inherit, with any conditions imposed, was laid down specifically by the terms of the will. The straw hat factory in Dunstable was to be offered to two employees, Thomas Weatherill and Richard Gutteridge, at valuation, each to have stock worth £1,000 if they accepted the offer. As the property remained in the possession of the Bennett family it appears that Mr Weatherill and Mr Gutteridge did not do so. Both men would have been getting on in years by this time and the hat trade was already declining. The factory was kept going by the family for some years, with Miss Rose Tibbett as the forewoman in the latter days, but more and more of the work was being transferred to Luton in the 1920s and it finally closed in 1931.

In memory of her husband Benjamin Bennett's widow donated money to Dunstable Council to be used for some sort of memorial to him. For over 20 years the Council had been discussing the desirability of providing a recreation ground for the town and it was decided to use the money to purchase the land for the Bennett Memorial Recreation Ground, in Bull Pond Lane, though it was not actually bought until 1920, after Mrs Bennett herself had died.

Mr and Mrs Stanley Bennett moved into Kensworth House and Mr Bennett ran the Estate from the office in High Street North, or perhaps it would be more accurate to say that his agents did. He and his wife always spent the winter months on the Sussex coast, returning to Kensworth only in the summer. The brewery and public houses were sold shortly before the Second World War, in 1938, to Mann, Crossman & Paulin. When the War began the Bennetts left Kensworth House and it was commandeered as a hostel for Land Army girls. Mr Stanley Bennett died in Wales in 1943 and his wife died a few years later. Kensworth House was put up for auction in 1946 and bought by Mr Bert England.

The new house built by Benjamin Bennett on the site of his father's house as it is today. The house on the right of it, now Town Hall Chambers, is very little changed apart from the shop fronts on the ground floor. (OR)

A few yards further along the High Street is No. 29, at present the Eleanor Gallery, the front of which was once part of Elliott's factory. From old photographs it appears that the original frontage was double the width of the present shop, the missing half being where Bar Chameleon is now. How much, if any, of the old building remains behind the facade today it is impossible to tell.

Some time early in the 19th century William Elliott the Younger, who had been born in Kent, where his father was an innkeeper, came back to the town from which his family originated. Like Benjamin Bennett he came here as a young man and, like him, courted and married the young widow of a hat manufacturer, Richard Hunter. She was still not quite 30, with a young daughter, and significantly she was also the daughter of another hat manufacturer, the William Oliver mentioned earlier. As a widow Mary Hunter, too, would have inherited her husband's estate, but although his factory is known to have been somewhere in the High Street it has not proved possible to find out exactly where. So it may, or may not, have been the building which was occupied by William Elliott later in the 1800s.

It is known that in 1795 William Elliott Senior bought from Mrs Ashton's executors the house next to the Crown, which would have been on the same site as the younger William Elliott's factory in the 19th century, but whether the factory was a new building or an adaptation of the old one is at present unclear. It is possible that Richard Hunter may have rented the premises from Mr Elliott Senior.

Before long young William had a thriving business, employing 90 hands, and like most of his fellow manufacturers was very involved in the concerns of the hat trade and the affairs of the town. He was elected to the first committee of the Straw Hat Manufacturers Association, was a founder member of the Mechanic's Institute and one of the first magistrates appointed when Dunstable was granted a commission of the peace, giving it the right to hold its own magistrates' courts, in 1866. No doubt he would have gone on to other offices had he lived longer, but he died at the age of 64, shortly after his appointment as a J.P.

After his death the firm went under the name of his widow, who seems to have played a large part in the business all her life, until about 1880, after which it became Elliott & Son. William Oliver Elliott was his parents' oldest son and followed his father into the business, apparently running it with his mother when his father first died but presumably gradually taking over the reins as his mother became older. Mary Elliott lived to be a grand old lady of ninety, remaining active to the end of her life, a matriarch presiding over her large family in her latter years. In business she must have been a redoubtable lady. Widely known and respected in the hat trade she was known in Luton as 'the Mother of Straw'.

Taken in 1934 this photograph shows Elliott's factory and Mr Warren's house next door virtually as they must have been at the end of the 19th century, apart from the shops on the ground floor. Mr Warren's house is the one towards the right of the picture, with the 'For Sale' board on it, and Elliott's factory is the long building on the left of it. (DG)

(Her second son, George, ran a hat factory in Luton.) She outlived her husband by nearly 30 years and her colleagues in the trade turned out in force for her funeral in January 1892. She was one of the few women in the town to be given a long and detailed obituary in the local paper.

A few months after her death her estate was put up for sale. The hat factory buildings had remained in her ownership and were not sold at the auction but were subsequently bought by her son. A year later he sold the premises again and retired from business. Part of the ground floor of the former factory then became a shop but eventually most of the building was demolished.

William Elliott and his wife, Charlotte, had a large family of eight boys and five girls. Two of the sons, David and William, were ordained as Church of England clergymen and a third, Percy, was a gifted musician who was a concert performer and at one time professor of the violin at the Royal Academy of Music. Like his father, William Elliott was appointed a Justice of the Peace and was very active in town affairs. Though he outlived his younger brothers he did not live to enjoy a long retirement. In 1902 he was staying with his son David in Sussex when he suffered a fatal heart attack. His obituary gives not a single detail of his family or his personal life but records that he was never known to speak an unkind word, was courteous and genial to everybody and always ready 'to relieve distress or remedy evils'.

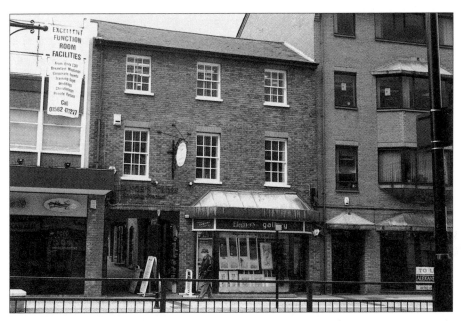

All that remains to be seen of Elliott's factory today is the upper part of No. 29 High Street North, now the Eleanor Gallery. (OR)

Next along the High Street today is a large brick office building, with shops/offices on the ground floor, numbered 31a and 31b. On this site once stood the Crown, an important coaching inn in its time, later to become the Crown hat factory for some seventy years.

After the inn was sold by the Burr family in 1843 it was occupied for several years by Thomas Squires, a bleacher, until William Milligan moved in in 1852. He had left his native Scotland to work in Dublin, and learn the linen trade, and from there his firm had sent him as a representative to Dunstable. He evidently decided that the hat trade offered good prospects and returned to form the partnership previously mentioned with Alexander Forfar. After about three years the two men parted company and in 1852 William moved a few doors along the road, to the former Crown, to set up in business on his own. The premises had by this time been adapted or extended and in addition to the living accommodation there were various workrooms and warehouses.

In the same year that he established his own business William Milligan also married Sophia Waterfield, one of the daughters of the hat manufacturer just across the road. Like his neighbours he found his business prospered and the number of workers in his factory grew from 30 in 1851 to almost a hundred in the 1870s, about the same number as were employed by Mr Bennett and Mr Elliott. He was soon accepted as one of the hat making fraternity who later would become a councillor, an alderman and, in 1870, the Mayor. He was a trustee of two of the town's biggest charities, a magistrate and a churchwarden of the parish church. He was described as a quiet, retiring sort of man, quite different from the extrovert Benjamin Bennett, but a man who worked diligently and conscientiously behind the scenes for the good of the town and the community.

Had he lived to a greater age he might well have expanded his business, but he died at the comparatively early age of 54, leaving his widow with four children, William, aged 19, and three girls whose ages ranged from 11 to 18. The firm continued in operation for a time, possibly with a manager, or possibly Sophia, coming from a hat manufacturing family, supervised it herself. Her mother and sisters were, after all, running a factory just across the road and would have been on hand to help and advise. The younger William Milligan did not follow his father into the firm but went instead to study at Cambridge and eventually, like some of the younger Bennetts and Elliotts, became a clergyman in the Church of England. His mother died only seven years after her husband, and the next year William and his sisters had moved to a house further along High Street North. The fixtures and fittings in the factory had been put up for auction soon after their mother's death and Matthew Walker, who had previously had factories in Church Street and Albion Street, had moved to the former Crown.

Matthew Walker, however, only stayed for about five years before selling out to Mr Alfred Warren, who had also had a factory in Albion Street for some 20 years or so. He had come here from London and by 1871 he, too, employed 80 hands. He left Albion Street in about 1885 and for some months afterwards an advertisement repeatedly appeared in the Dunstable Gazette for a tenant for 'a straw hat manufactory and two dwelling houses, late in the occupation of Alfred Warren'. But nobody took it on.

After the move Mr Warren immediately set about improving the living accommodation in High Street North and altered the appearance of the old inn by adding bay windows on the ground and first floor. (Bay windows were becoming fashionable in the High Street at this time.) The main part of the inn was now the Warrens' private house and was given the new name of Tresillian. The factory buildings were at the back of the house and Mr Warren had bought a strip of land behind the adjoining property to give him access to them from the rear without having to use the carriageway from the High Street for factory traffic.

Alfred Warren died in 1894 and his oldest son, another Alfred, took over the firm in Dunstable, while a younger brother, Edward Lonsdale, went to a second factory which had been opened in Bute Street in Luton. Although his father does not appear to have been involved in local affairs the younger Alfred became an alderman and was also a member of the local cricket club. His wife, too, was very active in local affairs and charity events, and one of her main concerns was the welfare of young women workers. She was made a J.P., and in 1931 was instrumental in setting up a school for young girls to be trained as milliners in an attempt to help the young women in the hat trade. She believed that they needed training to help them to compete with the London milliners.

Like all the other firms in the town, and in spite of branching out into the felt trade, Warren's was finding life difficult in the 1920s and towards the end of 1928 a notice appeared in the Hatters' Gazette to the effect that the Dunstable factory would shortly be closing and all the firm's operations transferred to their Luton factory, which was being extended. The writer commented that this was the only real factory left in Dunstable, as Bennett's 'were not maintaining a complete factory any longer'. In his latter days in Dunstable Mr Warren could be seen going off every morning, always immaculately dressed, with bowler hat, spats and umbrella, to catch the bus to Luton to go to work.

Two years after the closure at Dunstable Warren's amalgamated with a firm called Messrs Auburn Ltd., of 31 Maddox Street, London, but neither name appeared in the 1936 directory of Luton.

And also all that Messe or Tenement with the Stable Outbuildings heredits & appurts thereunto belonging site in Dunstable afsd formerly called or known by the name of the Windmill and Still Inn & now called the Crown Inn formerly in the occupon of Hannah Bisdaker Wo aftwds in the occupon of Thos Stokes late of Jo Smith deced then of Mary Smith his Widow then in the occupon of Walter Lloyd & as the same were then in the occupon of Squires.

And also all that other Messe or Tenement with the Stable Barns and piece of Land thereunto belonging with the appurts site in Dunstable afsd formerly in the occupon of Richd Hubbins aftwds of Thos Stokes since of Susan Goodman afterwds of Mark West late of Joseph Swift then of John Hall and late of James Maddocks and commonly called or known by the sign of the White Hart Inn.

An extract from the deeds of inns owned by Thomas Burr which were auctioned in 1843. It refers to the Crown, formerly the Windmill and Still, and the White Hart. (BLARS)

William Milligan, the founder of the Crown hat factory. (DTC)

In 1934 Tresillian was sold and the ground floor of the house became two shops, one of which was Bata shoe shop, still remembered by many Dunstablians. The house and much of the factory at the rear survived until, like Elliott's, they were demolished in the 1980s to make way for the Eleanor's Cross precinct and the office block on the High Street.

Alfred J Warren, the last owner of the Crown hat factory when it closed in 1928. (DG)

4. Taylor Brothers

Round the corner from the Crown factory, on the right hand side of Albion Street, is a building which has recently been refurbished, its brickwork painted white and the balconies outside the first floor windows painted blue, to match the fascias below. At street level are the Rendezvous Restaurant and the shop called Occasions (Nos 4-8). Adjoining it, and probably part of the same building originally, is what is now No. 2 Albion Street. From the 1870s to about 1915 Taylor Brothers manufactured hats in this building, though how much of it they occupied it is difficult to say. The archway through the middle of the building would have provided access for horses and wagons to the yard at the rear.

Taylor Brothers were a London firm with their headquarters in Wood Street, a street that was, with Aldermanbury, the centre of the straw hat trade in the City, and they also had a factory in Luton. They had a reputation for high-class workmanship and in 1878 they won a national award for some of their hats, manufactured in Dunstable, which are now in Luton Museum. For most of its existence the factory in Albion Street was managed by George Alfred Inwards (another member of the family was manager at Stuart & Sons', in High Street South, from the 1860s to the 1890s). It closed in about 1915 and the ground floor was turned into shops, one of which was a hat shop, Julia Peters, in the 1960s.

The building in Albion Street where Taylor Brothers had their hat factory. (OR)

5. Coopers'

Back in High Street North, just past the entrance to Manchester Place, is Cubes Night Club, previously a bingo hall and before that a cinema. There has been more than one building on this site in the last century, but in the second half of the 19th century Coopers' hat factory stood here for nearly 50 years.

It was in 1823, far from Dunstable, that a young man named John Cooper left his home in the village of Chedderton, in Staffordshire, and set out for Manchester where he was about to open a small draper's shop. He was later joined by his brother, George, and by the time they moved to larger premises in 1832 they had already become famous locally for straw plait and straw hats and their shop was known as 'Cooper's Straw Shop'. Eventually they gave up the retail trade to become wholesalers and, since they relied so much on Dunstable and Luton for their supplies, they decided to open a factory of their own in the area which would be supervised by John Cooper.

John must have been familiar with the area before he moved here because he had already married a young widow from Leighton Buzzard, Mary Ginger, in the late 1830s. Probably he had met her when he had been visiting firms in Dunstable and Luton on business, and as they both worshipped at the Methodist Church it seems likely that that is where they first became acquainted.

In 1843 Burr's brewery in High Street North, a large building which obviously had potential for conversion into a factory, was put up for sale. At the same time Thomas Burr's splendid house next to it, known as the Manor House (though there never was a real manor house in Dunstable) was to be auctioned. The Cooper Brothers bought the brewery and the house and John and his wife, Mary, moved south. Mary had been happy with her circle of friends in Manchester and in spite of having been brought up in Bedfordshire she did not want to come back to live here. Only the fact that she would be near to Beckerings Park, where she had grown up, partly reconciled her to the idea.

The brewery was converted into a hat factory which became the second largest in Dunstable. Outside the town the Coopers opened what they referred to as branches, probably sewing rooms, in Houghton Regis, Toddington, Markyate and Stanbridge. When all the employees were together there were some 300 people.

Both John and Mary Cooper were very active in the Methodist Church. John, like Benjamin Bennett, allowed Methodist preachers into his factory to address his workers and gave generously to the church fetes and bazaars. Mary Cooper took classes of young girls and undertook visiting in the villages. Two daughters were born while the couple lived here but Mary suffered continually from poor health and died when she was only 38, in 1851. She was buried in the churchyard of the Methodist Church at the Square and the gravestone is still there.

John Cooper stayed on in Dunstable for some years after his wife died. With William Elliott he was elected on to the committee of the Straw Hat Manufacturers Association and became one of the first magistrates appointed in the borough. Some time in the 1860s he returned to the North with his family and eventually re-married. On his retirement he left Manchester and went to live in Crieff, in Scotland, where he died in 1883.

The factory continued to operate until the mid 1870s, under a manager, finally closing between 1878 and 1884. The building stood empty for many years, a target for theft and vandalism, and in 1888 lead was stolen from the roof. The culprit was sentenced to a fine of £2 or 21 days in prison. There was an abortive attempt to sell it in 1894 but it remained in the Coopers' ownership for a number of years after that, before becoming the site of one of Dunstable's early cinemas.

The house was occupied by a succession of owners and tenants before the ground floor was turned into shops in 1926. The upper floors had already become a lodging house and by the time the building was demolished in 1963 it was in a very dilapidated state. A new General Post Office was built on the site which was closed in the 1990s, though the building remains.

Coopers' factory with the Manor House, where John Cooper and his family lived, on the right. The illustration is from Charles Lamborn's Dunstaplelogia, published in 1859. (BC)

John Cooper

George Cooper

James Gould Cooper

The three Cooper brothers. It was John who came to live in Dunstable and supervise the factory in High Street North. (MCL)

6. Waterfield's

From Cubes Night Club the trail crosses the High Street, to the Pizza Hut, next to the Sugar Loaf, which was once Waterfield's factory. William Waterfield had been a cordwainer, or shoemaker, who had come to Dunstable in the late 1700s and when he died in 1816 his widow and his oldest son, Thomas, set up as hat manufacturers in premises rented from the first William Elliott. Soon afterwards Thomas married Sophia and together they built up a successful business, helped later by their three daughters, Sarah, Sophia and Mary Ann.

After Thomas's early death at the age of 55, Sophia and her three daughters continued to run the factory between them and all went well for about 10 years, until the landlord sold the property to Joseph Osborn, owner of the draper's shop next door, who made it a condition of the purchase that the tenants should be given notice to quit. So late in 1851 or early in the next year the Waterfields moved to the factory next to the Sugar Loaf and it was soon after this that the middle daughter, Sophia, married William Milligan from across the road. The other two sisters, who never married, carried on the business with their mother, who died in 1880 and was remembered as a 'quiet and reticent lady' who was 'held in high esteem'. Sophia Milligan died in the same year as her mother and Sarah Waterfield in 1884, leaving Mary Ann, the youngest daughter, to carry on on her own. She retired in the mid-1890s and died in 1904.

At one time Mrs Waterfield, as Mr Warren was later to do, put in a planning application for bay windows on the front of the building. For some reason (perhaps because she was ahead of the fashion) this created a storm of protest and a very nasty letter appeared in the local paper condemning bay windows as being only for the 'whim and fancy of private individuals' being used 'to gaze and quiz at folks, especially on Sundays'. The members of the Council actually visited the premises to see if the windows really would, as was claimed, infringe on public rights, and one councillor was reported to have referred to such windows as 'unsightly projections'. In the end the Council refused the application and poor Mrs Waterfield did not get her bay windows. She wrote a charming letter of thanks to the Councillors who had supported her application which was printed in the Dunstable Gazette.

In the end, of course, the building, like so many others in the High Street, became a shop on the ground floor and the only new windows put in were shop windows. Durrant's furnishing shop moved in when the factory closed, followed in about 1956 by the Co-op and later by the Pizza Hut. Fortunately the appearance of the upper part of the building has not been altered and the typical hat factory windows are still there above the modern fascia.

The Pizza Hut was once Waterfield's hat factory. The typical hat factory windows on the upper floors remain unchanged. (OR)

On the other side of the Sugar Loaf, a few doors further along, are three shops now occupied by Oxfam, Help the Aged and the Halifax Building Society (Nos 36-40 High Street North). Standing on the pavement in front of them and looking at the three windows it is not immediately obvious that they are, in fact, all part of one building. But above the shops, as above the Pizza Hut, the rows of windows show that this, too, was a hat factory. It was built by James Blackwell and rented by the London firm of Woolley, Sanders from about 1858 onwards.

The firm was an old established company, originally known as Spurden, Woolley, Sanders & Co. They arrived here in the 1860s and rented the factory and manager's house which James Blackwell may have built for himself in the first instance. He was certainly living in that area in 1851 and it seems most unlikely that he would have provided such lavish accommodation if he had not intended to live there himself. Not only was the factory itself 'extensively and substantially built', with all the usual kinds of workrooms and offices, but the adjoining house and grounds were of a very superior standard and the manager must have thought himself well provided for. In the grounds there were tennis lawns, a conservatory, two greenhouses, kitchen gardens, a 'charming paddock', and fruit trees and ornamental shrubs, all enclosed by a high brick wall. The whole premises had been built, according to the auctioneer when they were sold in 1888, without regard for expense by 'our wealthy and respected old townsman'.

The factory and house had been put up for sale at the final settling of Richard and James Blackwell's estate and were sold for £2,300 to Mr Frederick Girling, a bank manager who may have been buying on behalf of Barclay's Bank. Woolley, Sanders, who rented them for £200 a year, stayed on as the tenants and later bought the property for themselves.

In 1927, with the hat trade by then in the doldrums, they decided that it was time to move out and concentrate all their production in this area in their Luton factory. They sold off the property and three shops were opened on the ground floor. Two of them became cafés – the Whipsiderry and the Central café – and the other was the Cycle & Wireless Shop, later Chattell's and then Weatherhead's and the Oxfam shop today.

This was Woolley Sanders' factory and the manager's house next door to it, in High Street North. The ground floor was converted into three shops in 1927. (OR)

Still further along, in the direction of the crossroads and just past the Nicholas Way entrance to the Quadrant shopping precinct, is a modern block consisting of two shops. The second, No. 22, stands empty at this moment, but it was here that James Jardine's hat factory stood in the 19th century. It was not one of the biggest, never employing more than about 50 hands, with a small, two-storey building facing on to the High Street in the front and some workshops behind.

Mr Jardine originated from Scotland, his migration to the south having been a gradual process, and he had worked at Dudley and at Birmingham before coming here. In 1845 he had taken premises in what was then Upper Houghton Regis, but would be part of Dunstable now, and moved to High Street North some time after 1850.

In those days the factory stood on the corner of a passage way called Houghton Lane, which led off the High Street along the side of a public house called the White Hart. It had been occupied previously by various tenants with connections with the hat trade, including the London firm of Gregory, Cubitt & Co., none of whom had stayed very long.

James and Amelia Jardine had 5 children, the youngest still only nine when James died, in 1860. The funeral of the 'respected manufacturer' was, we are told, 'of a truly impressive character', though the weather was 'unpropitious', which seems a slightly odd choice of word for such an occasion. With the help of the older children Amelia Jardine carried on the business, describing herself as a crinoline maker as well as a hat manufacturer in 1861, and the firm appeared in the directories as Jardine & Co. until the mid-1870s. Amelia Jardine retired soon afterwards and went to live on the opposite side of the road, and the last reference to the firm is an entry for James (the son of James and Amelia) as a hat manufacturer in 1885.

The former factory stood empty for a time and the ground floor of the building on the High Street was eventually divided into two, one half being occupied by an estate agent, J. H. Thorpe, and the other by Miss Biggs, a milliner. It was later made into one again and for many years was the office of the estate agents and auctioneers, Messrs Allcorn's. It was demolished when the Quadrant shopping precinct was built in the 1960s.

A photograph of a parade of Dunstable cadets, taken in the 1950s, showing what had been the Jardines' house a century before. The low building, with the double fronted shop at ground level, was by this time Allcorn's, estate agents and auctioneers. It was between the White Hart and what is now the Nationwide Building Society. (DG)

9. Collings'

Next door to the empty No. 22 High Street North is the Nationwide Building Society, once the home of two generations of the Collings family. Born in Leighton Buzzard, Thomas George Collings settled in Dunstable as a young man and uniquely combined being a watch and clockmaker with being a straw hat manufacturer. Land Tax records show that he bought the house now occupied by the Building Society in 1821/2 and many years later he also acquired the one next door, now No. 18 and currently empty. There were two acres of land at the back, on part of which the factory buildings stood.

Thomas George and Mary Collings had five children, one of them a son whom they called, somewhat confusingly, Thomas George. He was to follow his father into the hat manufacturing business and also appears to have been, for a time, a jeweller, though not a watchmaker. Thomas George Senior always carried on his two trades simultaneously. He is recorded as having repaired the workhouse clock at Dunstable and the church clock at St. Mary's, Eaton Bray, and at least one clock made by him is known to be still in existence and in the possession of a local resident. In his later years he left his son to carry on hat manufacturing while he concentrated entirely on watch and clockmaking. He and his wife also left the house to the younger Thomas George and his large household of six children, a governess, a nursemaid and a cook, with two warehouse assistants also living in, and moved to Rose Cottage, in the northern end of the town. He died in 1866, three years after the death of his wife.

In the 1870s the Collings firm was of a moderate size, employing 70 women, and Thomas Junior's son, Montague, was still only in his teens. To begin with he went into the business with his father but later moved to Luton to set up on his own, eventually leaving the district altogether. For a time after his father's death the High Street North factory appeared in the directories under the name of Mrs Thomas George Collings. There were no other sons to follow on, for all of the other children in the family were girls.

Though the 1890 directory includes the firm under Mrs Collings' name it must, by then, have closed or been on the verge of closing. In June of that year the property was put up for sale in two lots, the house and the factory being offered separately. By now the house had been named Collingwood House and it included a dining room, a large front room used as a show room, a library, an upstairs drawing room and seven bedrooms, besides all the usual offices. According to the estate agent it could, with a 'small outlay', be reconverted into two dwellings.

However, the house, at any rate, was not sold, and when Mrs Collings died in 1893 it was still mortgaged. It was not until 1914 that it was sold by order of the mortgagees and bought by an estate agent, Thomas Thorne. No. 18 became first the London & County Bank, then a post office, then a cinema and afterwards the Confectionery Bazaar, still there in living memory. The last long-term occupant was the electrical goods retailer Curry's. No. 20 was used successively as the residence of the bank manager, the postmaster and the manager of the cinema. After it was acquired by Thomas Thorne it became a hat shop before being Charlie Cole's cycle shop, and in the 1980s it was taken over by the Nationwide Building Society.

The present Nationwide Building Society and the boarded-up shop to the right were both owned by the Collings family and their factory was behind them. (OR)

Over the crossroads, beside the little passage way on the left leading down to the Priory Church, is the William Hill betting shop, at No 17 High Street South. Those who care to look up to the top of the building will see the name Albion Buildings above the top windows. This was the house built by Mr Osborn, the draper, on the site of the factory where the Waterfields had first started making hats. When it was first built Mr Osborn himself lived there, with some of the assistants in his draper's shop living in, a common practice in those days.

When the time came for him to retire he had the house made into two shops, each with living accommodation, which were let to tenants, and he retired to Hastings. The International Tea Company Limited, to give it its full title, took up the tenancy of one and William Francis, an ironmonger, took the other. Eventually the International took over both shops and finally bought the whole building.

Albion Buildings, occupied on the ground floor by William Hill, were built on the site of Waterfield's first hat factory. (OR)

Past the next row of shops is Priory House, next to the gates leading into the Priory Gardens. For most of the 19th century it would not have been possible to see the Church from the High Street; the gardens were privately owned, Priory House was the residence of the manager of Munt & Brown's hat factory and the factory itself blocked the view from the street.

Munt & Brown's main warehouse, like Taylor Brothers', was in Wood Street, in London. They were the first of the London firms to establish a branch in Dunstable, taking a lease on Priory House in about 1833. A picture of Priory House painted c1812 shows a two-storey annex on the south side of the building, which was probably used initially as the hat factory, while the factory manager lived in the house itself. In 1839 Munt & Brown bought the property and it may well have been at this time that the annex was extended and another storey added. Munt & Brown was to become the largest firm in the town, at one time employing more workers here than in their factory at Luton. 350 women and 40 men were working there in 1864, compared with 200 women and 15 men at Luton.

Priory House, home of the managers of Munt & Brown's, in High Street South. (DTC)

Being in charge of such a large establishment gave their managers a certain status in the community and they joined the local owners in activities on a more or less equal footing. Like Mr & Mrs Bennett and Mr & Mrs Cooper, the managers and their wives arranged 'treats' for their workers and they organised sports events in competition with the Luton factory. For decades the firm was regarded as one of the 'leading and most stable firms in the straw hat industry'.

In the course of time the company went on to buy several other properties in the town. At one time they owned the land on which the Little Theatre stands today, which they sold to the Chew's Foundation to enable them to build additional accommodation for Chew's School. They bought what has become the Downtown Café, apparently originally as a residence for one of their staff, and they owned the house occupied at one time by the Alfred House Academy, afterwards advertised as being suitable for a straw manufacturer.

Because Munt & Brown had always been regarded as such a stable company it was all the more shocking when, in July 1908, their creditors received a letter informing them that 'Mr Harry Brown, trading as Munt & Brown, found himself unable to continue the business', and were requested to send their accounts in to the accountants.

A meeting of the creditors was held in London on 28th July 1908, when the chief creditor recounted the events which had led up to what he referred to as 'this sad occasion'. Sixty years earlier a partnership had existed between Richard Munt, three members of the Brown family (father and two sons) and a Mr Albert Langmore. By 1894 Mr Munt, Mr Brown Senior and Mr Langmore had all died, the latter owing the firm £20,000 at the time of this death. Mr Thomas Brown had also left the company after a dispute over a debt of £40,000 which he owed the company and had had no further connection with it.

These events had left Mr Harry Brown, the only member of the original partnership left in the firm, struggling on alone, hoping to return the firm to a state of solvency. He had actually put money of his own, from other sources, into the company to try and save it. He was now 72 and feeling he could no longer carry on had reluctantly called a meeting of his creditors. His one and only wish was to see that the company's assets were realised to the best advantage and to pass on to the creditors every penny raised.

His fellow manufacturers obviously had an enormous respect for him and he was given a standing ovation. It was agreed that the company's affairs should be dealt with under a deed of assignment and the meeting closed with a vote of sympathy for Mr Brown.

So it was that Arthur Munt, youngest son of Mr Munt, came to live in Priory House in Dunstable. Possibly he had accepted the house as his share of the estate due to him under the terms of his father's will, or he may have bought it when the company's assets were sold off. One of the first things he did after moving in was to arrange for the demolition of the factory next door, which actually came down in 1909 though the front wall was left standing up to about first-floor level, with a gateway through to the garden, for many years. Mr Munt became a familiar figure walking along the High Street, smoking his pipe, with his 'faithfully attendant terriers' trotting along behind him. He died in 1927, but his widow lived on in the house until about 1945. It was then bought by Dunstable Council and used by them as offices, but was sold to a commercial company after the town became part of the South Bedfordshire District in the local government re-organisation of 1973. At the time of writing it is hoped that the house, with a long history going back to medieval times, will soon belong to Dunstable once again.

View of Priory House from the Priory Gardens. (DTC)

70

An advertisement for Munt & Brown's hats from a trade journal. (LM)

Along past the Saracen's Head, opposite to Friar's Walk, is the Downtown Café (No. 59 High Street South). Very probably it had started life as the Star Inn, but if so it had long been a private house and the name transferred elsewhere when Eliza Osborne moved in. At that time it belonged to Munt & Brown and the previous tenant had been George Horn, a plait dealer, who had been declared bankrupt. In August 1870 it was advertised to rent, with immediate occupation, and described as being suitable for a straw manufacturer. Eliza was then carrying on her business in the house next door and decided to move.

Unfortunately we know very little about her. When Thomas Bagshawe bought the house in 1923 he found a photograph, dating from about 1870, of a group of people standing in front of the building. Most of them are obviously workers from the factory, but two of the women in the picture are better dressed than the others and standing slightly apart, so was one of them Eliza herself? There is nothing on the back of the picture to give us any clues as to who any of the people were and we can only speculate, but it does seem to be a distinct possibility. Eliza was born in Dunstable, the daughter of James, a wheelwright, and his wife Elizabeth, and began working as a bonnet sewer. Her factory was small, probably never employing more than about 20 hands. She retired in about 1880, or a little earlier, and went to live at No. 8 Icknield Street, accompanied by the lady who had been her chief assistant at the factory. (Perhaps the other lady on the left in the photograph?) She never married and there was only a brief announcement in the deaths column of the local paper when she died in 1884.

Back in 1872 the house in High Street South had been sold by Munt & Brown, probably to John Twidell, of Caddington, but Eliza remained as the tenant, paying an annual rent of £30. When she retired John Twidell's widow moved into the house with her two youngest daughters, Flora and Julia. Flora married Richard Blackwell, from across the road, but Julia never married and moved elsewhere after her mother died.

It must have been a large house for a household of only three women and a servant. It consisted of a basement, the ground floor, a first floor with four bedrooms and a large second floor. Up on this top floor Mr Bagshawe discovered there was a large room which was still partitioned off into 7 small workrooms, just as it must have been in Eliza Osborne's day, unaltered by any of the occupants who had lived there since she left.

Some time early in the 20th century someone had painted the house grey and it was as The Grey House that it was known for many years. It became the Grey House Hotel in 1952 and in more recent times has been re-named the Downtown Café.

Eliza Osborne's factory in about 1870. It is possible that one of the ladies on the left of the photograph was Eliza herself. The house was later known as The Grey House. (DTC)

The Downtown Café. Eliza Osborne's former factory as it is today. (PB)

Across the road from the Downtown Café, slightly further along the road, is Viceroy Court, but as recently as the early 1960s there were two large houses where the modern flats are today. One was Glenlossie, once the home of Francis Horn, the plait dealer, and the other was Avon Lodge, for a hundred years the home of the Blackwell family.

Richard Blackwell, a Northamptonshire man, came to live at Avon Lodge and built his hat factory behind the house. He was one of the early arrivals in the trade in the 19th century and by 1809 he had met and married a local girl, Ann Sharman. Two years later they had a son, James William, who joined his father in the business as a young man. He, in turn, also married a local girl, Rebecca Oliver (sister of Mrs Elliott) and by 1841 there were two Blackwell establishments in the town, one in High Street South and one in High Street North.

One of the Blackwells is said by Charles Lamborn to have invented a new way of making straw plait by working the straws inside out, so that the inner side of the straw was exposed. It was known as rice straw plait because of its special, delicate colour, and the hats made from it were very much favoured for weddings, at a cost of one guinea.

The Blackwells must have been one of the most successful families in the business and by 1861, when James was still only 50, both father and son had retired and were of independent means. James had had a large factory built in High Street North about ten years earlier, the one rented by Woolley, Sanders, and was living nearby. A few years on both Richard and James had died, Richard in 1863 and James in 1868, which seems to have caused some problems with probates and the execution of the wills. Twenty years after James's death the Court of Chancery ruled that some of the property owned by them should be sold by public auction in order to make a final settlement of the estate. Apart from the factory in High Street North, other properties sold included the house on the corner of Albion Street, which later became the Gazette Office, together with the house behind it, which went for £1,110, and two three-storey houses in Albion Street. The total proceeds were over £4,000. One point of interest concerning Richard Blackwell's will is that one of the executors was Frederick Sanders, of Wood Street, London, so there was obviously some other connection between the Blackwells and Woolley, Sanders besides the renting of the factory in High Street North.

James Blackwell had moved into Avon Lodge after his father's death and his son, Richard James, lived there to the end of his life. He was the Mr Blackwell who married Flora Twidell from over the road. They had one daughter, Phyllis, who suffered from poor health and died young. Richard never worked for a living, was never a councillor, and his name rarely appeared in the Dunstable Gazette. He occasionally opened the grounds of his house for some special event – a brass band competition, to which admission cost sixpence, was one – but he was not a public man.

The factory at the back of the house was eventually made into another house for someone else in the family, and The Chestnuts now stands in what was part of the original grounds of Avon Lodge. Richard Blackwell died in 1916 and Flora in 1931. Avon Lodge was sold and remained a private residence until the 1960s.

Richard James Blackwell and his wife, Flora. (EB)

The back of Blackwell's factory after it had been converted into a private house. Viceroy Court has now been built on the site. (EB)

Back along the road towards the crossroads, in the Square, is Norton House (No 52 High Street South), now used as offices, where the manager of Stuart & Sons once lived. The firm of Stuart & Taylor opened a factory here in about 1863. Later on they became Stuart & Sons, a London firm with a head office in Old Change, London, but whether or not there was any connection between the original firm and Taylor Brothers has not been discovered.

The factory was behind the house on the Square and the whole property was owned by the Revd. Thomas Gostelow Lockhart, possibly through an inheritance. It was still being extended in 1887 and the planning application can still be seen in the County Record Office. The Revd. Lockhart died in 1906 and his executors put the property up for auction, but it failed to reach the reserve price, although the factory was described as 'commodious and extensive' and the manager's house as 'high-class'.

Stuart & Sons continued to manufacture hats there until 1925, when they closed the factory. For many years after that the buildings were occupied by an engineering company, until the re-development of that part of the town a few years ago. There is one small part of the old factory buildings that still remains, just beyond the archway which leads to the modern flats today, on the left-hand side. In the whole of its existence there were only ever two managers of the factory - John Inwards, who died in 1898 and Alfred Lovell, who died in 1934, aged 77.

Norton House, facing on to The Square, an 18th century house that was once the home of the managers of Stuart & Sons' factory. (OR)

INDEX OF NAMES

KEY TO SOURCES OF ILLUSTRATIONS

BC	The Book Castle	7b, 57
BLARS	Bedfordshire & Luton Archives and Records Service	43, 53a
DG	Dunstable Gazette	23, 35, 49, 54, 64
DTC	Dunstable Town Council	7a, 9, 27, 45, 53b, 68, 70, 73
EB	Mrs Elsie Buck	76, 77
LM	Luton Museum	11, 15, 17, 19, 21, 29, 31, 33, 71
MCL	Manchester Central Library	58
MD	Mrs Mary Dolman	37
OR	Mr Omer Roucoux	47, 50, 55, 60, 62, 66, 67, 79
PB	Mr Philip Belding	74

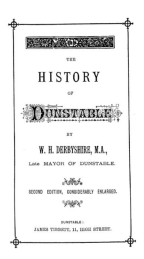

THE
HISTORY
OF
DUNSTABLE
BY
W. H. DERBYSHIRE, M.A.,
Late MAYOR OF DUNSTABLE.

SECOND EDITION, CONSIDERABLY ENLARGED.

DUNSTABLE:
JAMES TIBBETT, 11, HIGH STREET.

THE HISTORY OF DUNSTABLE
by
W.H. Derbyshire M.A.

This is the third in the Book Castle series of reprints of fascinating old books about Dunstable. Published as collector's editions in handsome bindings, with a new preface by John Buckledee.

William Derbyshire was one of the town's most influential and controversial figures in the centre of public affairs.

A Book Castle Publication

THE
DUNSTAPLELOGIA:
WHEREIN IS SET FORTH, THE
ORIGIN, MANNERS, CUSTOMS, TRADE
AND PROGRESS,
OF THE
TOWN OF DUNSTAPLE,
WITH NUMEROUS ILLUSTRATIONS,
AND THE ANTIQUITIES CONNECTED THEREWITH
DURING THE
ROMAN AND SAXON PERIODS,
WITH MANY TRANSLATIONS FROM THE ORIGINAL LATIN;
BY
CHARLES LAMBORN,
LATE HEAD MASTER OF THE BRITISH SCHOOL, DUNSTAPLE, AND
POPULAR LECTURES IN NATURAL PHILOSOPHY.

DUNSTAPLE:
PRINTED AND PUBLISHED
BY JAMES TIBBETT, "ALBION" PRINTING OFFICE, HIGH STREET.
1859.

THE DUNSTAPLELOGIA
by
Charles Lambourn

This unique history of Dunstable is published by the Book Castle as the second in its series of new editions of rare books about the town.

The Dunstaplelogia, one of the earliest attempts to recount the history of Dunstable in some sort of scholarly order, included a number of beautiful engravings of local buildings, based on the work of a "photographic artist", James Tibbett Jnr, who was the son of the book's original publisher.

A Book Castle Publication

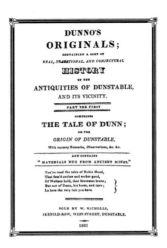

DUNNO'S ORIGINALS;

CONTAINING A SORT OF

REAL, TRADITIONAL, AND CONJECTURAL

HISTORY

OF THE

ANTIQUITIES OF DUNSTABLE,

AND ITS VICINITY.

PART THE FIRST

COMPRISES

THE TALE OF DUNN;

OR THE

ORIGIN OF DUNSTABLE,

With cursory Remarks, Observations, &c. &c.

AND CONTAINS

" MATERIALS DUG FROM ANCIENT MINES."

You're read the tales of Robin Hood,
That fam'd outlaw and archer good,
Of Wallace bold, that Scotsman brave;
But not of Dunn, his horse, and cave;
Lo here the very tale you have.

SOLD BY W. NICHOLLS,
IKENILD-ROW, WEST-STREET, DUNSTABLE.

1821

DUNNO'S ORIGINALS
The First Complete Edition

A facsimile of five booklets concerning the history of Dunstable and its vicinity, including Totternhoe, Eaton Bray, Toddington, Flitwick and Flitton, first published in 1821 and 1822. Also four similar, rediscovered, and newly set manuscripts, completed by the author in 1823 shortly before his death, but previously unpublished. New introduction and glossary by John Buckledee, editor of the Dunstable Gazette.

The
Book
Castle

A Book Castle Publication

Dunstaple: A Tale of the Watling Highway
The legend of Dunne the Robber

by

A.W.Mooring

Dunstaple…a dramatic historical romance, which will particularly fascinate anyone interested in the legends of Dunstable's past. The story is woven around the tale of Dunne the Robber, the man whose exploits were said by some to be the basis for the town's modern name.

A.W.Mooring, editor of The Dunstable Borough Gazette between 1895 and 1909, took the gist of the legend about the outlaws who infested the forests around Dunstable crossroads in the time of King Henry 1, and added a romantic tale set among the Totternhoe caverns and the ramparts of Maiden Bower.

It first appeared as a six-month serial in The Gazette in 1898 and the following year in two different hardback editions produced in the newspaper's printing works in Albion Street, Dunstable.

Unavailable ever since, it is now published in facsimile by The Book Castle of Dunstable with the addition of a reface by John Buckledee, the present editor of The Gazette.

A Book Castle Publication

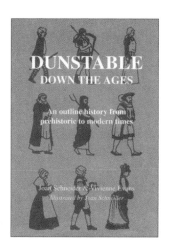

DUNSTABLE DOWN THE AGES
An outline history from prehistoric to modern times
by
Joan Schneider & Vivienne Evans

People have lived in South Bedfordshire for thousands of years, even before the Romans constructed Watling Street, and a town grew up where Dunstable now stands on the crossing with the Icknield Way.

Then came Anglo-Saxon immigrants, and the creation of a new town and a Priory by Henry 1. There was a royal residence, and a Queen Eleanor cross was built, after her coffin rested at the Priory. The decision, which ended Henry V111's first marriage and caused England's break with the Roman Catholic Church, was taken here. The following century saw religious controversy causing violent clashes in Dunstable.

Almshouses and schools were founded on the proceeds of distilling gin. Long distance coaches appeared on improved roads, and inns for travellers, but there were highwaymen too. Straw bonnets sold to travellers started the hat trade, which flourished in Victorian times. All these aspects are covered in this valuable publication.

A Book Castle Publication

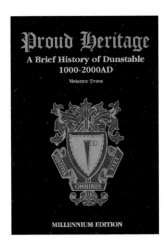

PROUD HERITAGE
A brief history of Dunstable 1000-2000AD
by
Vivienne Evans

Dunstable was founded by a king, had a palace, a very important Augustinian Priory and until 1600 was visited by nearly every king and queen of England. Sited on the crossroads less than forty miles from London, Oxford and Cambridge, Dunstable has been involved in many national events. Its populace has had to face economic and religious upheavals, but time after time Dunstablians pulled together, changed direction and won through to another successful era. Devoting a chapter to each of the ten centuries of the millennium, this book first sets the national and county scene in order to make more comprehensible the purely Dunstable events. Included in this book are stories about the Priory Church, Priory House, Kingsbury, Grove House, the Sugar Loaf and other inns, Ashton St Peter and other schools. Middle Row, Edward Street and other roads, the straw hat industry and the growth of the town.

A Book Castle Publication

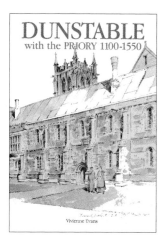
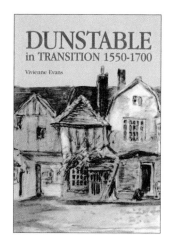

DUNSTABLE with the PRIORY 1100-1550
by
Vivienne Evans

This is the dramatic story of Henry I's busy and influential town with its royal palace, Augustinian Priory, Dominican Friary and thriving businesses around a major crossroads. Its rapid rise to success sees it linked to many famous national issues such as Magna Carta, the Eleanor Crosses, the Peasants' Revolt, the annulment of Henry VIII's marriage and the dissolution of the monasteries.

DUNSTABLE in TRANSITION 1550-1700
by
Vivienne Evans

The residents of Dunstable needed all their resourcefulness to rebuild the town's success without the Augustinian Priory. Though disrupted by civil war, the developing coaching industry soon filled Dunstable with inns, as some new visitors brought wealth and importance to counterbalance other travellers who posed problems of poverty and disease. The age's religious upheavals found a microcosm in Dunstable. The majority stayed worshipping at the Priory Church, but some left for America and others met in secret until reform led to the acceptance of Quakers and Baptists. Scandal punctuated this period of turmoil - the baptism of a sheep at church, the hounding of a suspected witch and the predations of notorious highwaymen. All elements of Dunstable in a volatile, transitional phase.

A Book Castle Publication

DUNSTABLE SCHOOL
1888-1971
by
F.M. Bancroft

"It was not one of the leading schools in the country…But it was a grammar school, a good grammar school, and it gave a sound all round education aligned with sporting activities of note. It taught courtesy, politeness and the home truths of life. And because of the masters over the years and a lot of the boys who went there it was a character school, with a happy atmosphere."

So, for all these reasons along with their own personal memories, though the school was superseded over a generation ago thousands of Old Boys still remember it with deep affection and gratitude.

A Book Castle Publication

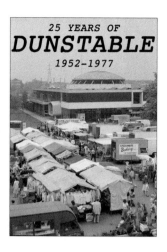

25 YEARS OF DUNSTABLE 1952-1977
A collection of photographs
by
Bruce Turvey

An era of enormous change in the town, 1952-1977, is commemorated in this superb collection of over 400 photographs – the best from Bruce Turvey's professional collection of over 100,000. Originally published to mark the Queen's Silver Jubilee, her Golden Jubilee seems a fitting moment for its re-issue.

Changes include the disappearance of key old landmarks such as the Town Hall, the Red Lion and the California swimming pool, as well as the opening of the prestigious Civic (Queensway) Hall, the circular Catholic Church and the Quadrant Shopping Centre. Here are glimpses of other outstanding occasions, including Whipsnade's 21st Birthday party, the Pageant depicting 750 years of town history, and the granting of the Freedom of the Borough to the Herts and Beds Yeomanry – six years before the town's loss of that status in 1974.

Famous visitors abound – four Prime Ministers, along with personalities like Kenneth More, Arthur Askey, David Kossoff, Brenda Lee, George Best, Mary Peters, Hugh Gaitskell and the Duchess of Gloucester. And of course there are hundreds of local people pictured in the photographs of sports teams, coach outings, dinner dances, carnival floats, retirement parties and uniformed organisations.

The book opens with a snow scene and closes with a heat wave. In between are the myriad events that comprise the life of a market town during three different decades a generation ago.

A Book Castle Publication

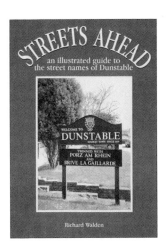

STREETS AHEAD
An Illustrated Guide to the Street Names of Dunstable
by
Richard Walden

Over the past 150 years Dunstable has expanded from a small rural market town with limited development beyond the four main streets, to a modern urban town of 35,000 inhabitants and over 300 individual streets.

The names of many of those streets have been carefully chosen for some specific reason. Dunstable's modern housing estates in particular have been spared the all too common anonymity of poets, painters, authors and birds found in most other town. In Dunstable, developers and the local Council have taken great care to select names, which record elements of the town's unique historical past and some of the characters and events, which helped to shape the local community.

Streets Ahead is extensively illustrated with hundreds of photographs and copies of original documents, many of which have never been published before. The content of this work also makes it a fascinating record of the town's recent history.

A Book Castle Publication

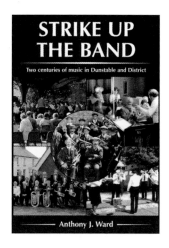

STRIKE UP THE BAND
Two centuries of music in Dunstable and District
by
Anthony J.Ward

In 'Strike Up The Band', the Author traces the history of music making in Dunstable and District from the earliest times where information is available, up to the present day. It is derived from a wider ongoing project by the author.

The book particularly emphasises the history and development of Brass Bands, Orchestras and other groups, recording their contributions to the changing life of the Town and District, and highlighting the various celebrations that have taken place over so many years. The book closes with a series of chapters on the three local Senior Schools in Dunstable with their bands, orchestras and music.

The design of the book is largely based on a collection of photographs and memorabilia, derived from the wide number of contributors having connections with the organisations featured in the book, featuring their recollections of events and personalities. The story of music making in Dunstable and its surrounding villages is shown in the context of the history of the area and its citizens.

A Book Castle Publication